USEFUL REFERENCE SERIES NO. 84

The Pamphlet File

IN SCHOOL, COLLEGE, AND PUBLIC LIBRARIES

Revised and Enlarged
Edition

By
NORMA OLIN IRELAND
Author, *The Picture File;*
Index to Monologs and Dialogs; Index to Indexes
Editor, *Local Indexes in American Libraries*

BOSTON
F. W. FAXON COMPANY, INC.
1954

TO *My Aunt,* Belle Latimer Wall
and
The Memory of *My Uncle,* Jay Monroe Latimer

"Flower in the crannied wall,
I pluck you out of the crannies,
I hold you here, root and all, in my hand,
Little flower — but if I could understand
What you are, root and all, and all in all,
I should know what God and man is."
— ALFRED, LORD TENNYSON

FOREWORD

This work is a revision of the earlier volume, *The Pamphlet File,* published in 1937. It has been undertaken at the request of the Publishers, due to the continuance of orders for the book since the first edition has been exhausted.

The Pamphlet File was originally written as a companion volume to *The Picture File,* which is also available in a revised and enlarged edition, reissued in 1952. As in the case of the previous volume, the purpose of our work is to compile a simple guide suitable for the average school, college and public library, using methods and subject headings which have proved their usefulness. Since the publication of our first edition, we have had the privilege of working with pamphlet collections in three other libraries: a small college, a medium-sized public, and a large university. We have observed and studied many other collections and thus feel that our new work is based on a much wider background of experience than our earlier work.

We have added over 600 new headings, including up-to-date geographical names and current subjects, bringing the total number of subjects to over 2,000. We have greatly expanded our "Subdivisions for Local Material" and have given it new importance in a separate supplement (SUP—PLEMENT I). We have combed current library literature for articles on pamphlets, and have included pertinent quotations from magazines of the last few years. We have re-arranged and re-written our text, and included a new section on Propaganda. We wish to thank Senator Nelson S. Dilworth, State Senator of California, for reading this section.

A completely new feature of this revised edition is our "Partial List of Organizations, etc. That Issue Pamphlets" found in SUPPLEMENT II. Over 660 names are included in this list. For explanation of classes of organizations included, see explanation in Chapter I, p. 2. We mailed hundreds of cards to organizations and in most cases the response was excellent, enabling us to examine representative pamphlets of a great many of the agencies listed. To make this list doubly useful, we have compiled a "Subject Index" to these organizations, including over 350 representative subjects. We believe this list will enable the pamphlet librarian to build a pamphlet collection of recent material, although it is not intended to be complete. Subjects indexed, however, are found in our "List of Subject Headings" and therefore constitute a good beginning for any up-to-date pamphlet file. We urge forbearance, however, in ordering from this list, as pamphlets go out of print quickly, and organizations do not always respond to requests. We have tried to check the latest addresses, in all cases, but changes are constantly being made.

We have spent some little time compiling a usable list of "Bibliographical Sources of Pamphlets" which is a new feature of our work, found on p. 3. Included is a list of "Periodicals with Pamphlet Lists," which although by no means comprehensive, yet we believe it to be unique as we know of no similar list in print. The pamphlet librarian can easily expand this list, according to the periodicals received in his particular library.

We wish to thank Mrs. Martha Westwood and Mrs. Vowyla Threlkeld of the Glendale Public Library for their special interest in this work and for their kindness in making their library resources easily available. We also thank Mrs. Thelma Jackman and her assistants in the Sociology department of the Los Angeles Library and Miss Florence Powers and others of the Reference department of the Pasadena Library for their fine service.

Again may we say that the resourcefulness of the individual librarian is all-essential, and the successful use of this book is dependent on its application to local problems and needs.

N. O. I.

TABLE OF CONTENTS

CHAPTER I

How to Begin

"What shall I do with pamphlets" is usually the problem of the librarian, rather than "How shall I 'go about' getting them?" The necessity of a pamphlet file is often thrust upon a library because of the gradual and steady accumulation of this sort of material, increasingly important in this day and age. Students and adults alike are demanding the latest information on subjects and do not care to wait for books to be published. For the small library whose magazine resources are small, and also for the large library whose demands are necessarily greater, a pamphlet file is an absolute necessity.

1. SELECTION

A careful and consistent policy of pamphlet selection however, is very important. We are inclined to agree with the librarian who describes the typical vertical file of yesterday like this: [1] "I believe I speak for the mass of reference librarians when I say that the typical vertical file is a collection that 'just growed.'" But we believe that this is not true of today's vertical file because librarians are now more conscious that selection of pamphlets is just as important as the selection of books, and that a careful study and use of pamphlet-selection tools is extremely important.

For this purpose, therefore, we have made a selective study of pamphlet sources, both primary and secondary, and offer these to our readers. We have not intended to make an exhaustive list, impractical because of the limits of this work, but rather a good beginning list for the librarian to carry on and complete. In addition to these bibliographic sources, we have also compiled a "PARTIAL LIST OF ORGANIZATIONS, ETC. THAT ISSUE PAMPHLETS," located in Supplement II.

---

[1] Esterquest, Ralph T. Pressure groups in your pamphlet file. *Library Journal* 64: 226, March 15, 1939

1

"Partial List"

There are over 660 organizations listed in Supplement II, which is only a partial list of the many thousands of companies that issue material. Our basis for inclusion was determined by a representative coverage of subjects and types of organizations, including many corporations and companies not easily found elsewhere. Lack of space made it advisable to exclude large groups of organizations found in other lists (such as in *World Almanac,* Judkins' *National Associations of U. S., American Booktrade Directory, Public Affairs Information Service,* and special directories), with of course some exceptions. For instance we have omitted the majority of: 1. Travel agencies (list available in our *Picture File,* p. 3–5) ; 2. Picture agencies (*Picture File,* p. 6–9) ; 3. Book publishers (in *U. S. Catalog; American Booktrade Directory*) ; 4, 5, 6, 7, Religious societies, Foundations, Political organizations, Educational associations (found in various periodical indexes). We have not included many college and university presses, except for extension work, and agricultural colleges. There are some few exceptions to the above omissions where names have been included in our list because of their special pamphlet coverage. Compared with 4,000 trade, professional, civic and other associations included in Judkins' work, however, our small list of over 660 can only be called a "Partial List."

"Subject Index"

In connection with our "Partial List of Organizations . . ." we have added a new feature which we hope will be of real value. This is a "Subject Index," covering a sampling of pamphlet subjects issued by these organizations. It should be useful not only to librarians who want to bring their files up-to-date with good, new material, but also to librarians who wish to start a pamphlet file.

We repeat, however, that we give no "blanket endorsement" to all pamphlets published by all agencies listed, because it was physically impossible to examine all publications issued by these agencies.

The main tools of pamphlet buying are, of course, the

published bibliographical sources: *Comprehensive publication lists, Pamphlet services, Periodicals and their indexes, Federal and State government document lists, Published bibliographies of pamphlets.* We shall try to outline these Bibliographical Sources at this time.

2. BIBLIOGRAPHICAL SOURCES OF PAMPHLETS

I. COMPREHENSIVE PUBLICATION LISTS

1. Publisher's Weekly. R. R. Bowker Co., 62 W. 45th St., N. Y. 19, N. Y. Weekly. (Pamphlets below the line. Probably second most comprehensive list issued.)
2. U. S. Copyright Office. Pamphlets, serials, and contributions to periodicals. Third series, Part 1B. U. S. Copyright Office. Semi-annual. (Most comprehensive list. Usable if you know the author or agency, but not for casual buying.)

II. PAMPHLET SERVICES

1. Bacon Pamphlet Service, Inc., 273 New York Ave., Huntington, N.Y. (Clearing house for all publications in paper covers, such as American Recreation series, etc.)
2. The Pamphleteer Monthly. The William-Frederick Press; Pamphlet Distributing Co., 313 W. 35th St., N. Y. 1, N. Y. ("A Buying-Guide to Worthwhile Reading." A central agency to supply the pamphlets and books listed in each issue.)
3. The Vertical File Service Catalog. H. W. Wilson Co., 950 University Ave., N. Y. 52, N. Y. Monthly. ("Pamphlets listed in this Catalog should be ordered from their publishers or sources which are given in the entries.")

III. PERIODICALS AND THEIR INDEXES

The special periodical indexes are valuable for "continuation" pamphlet publications such as Proceedings, Reports, Yearbooks. Documents on special subjects can also be selected from such indexes, as well as Extension and Experiment Station publications and occasional literature. Such indexes include: Agriculture Index; Bibliographic Index; Education Index; Industrial Arts Index; Occupational Index; Public Affairs Information Service.

PERIODICALS WITH PAMPHLET LISTS

This is by no means a complete list, but we believe that no other similar list exists at this time. Inclusion was based on two main factors: regular listing which included a sizable number of pamphlets, and availability of magazines as judged by representative libraries in area. We do not, however, give a blanket endorsement to all pamphlets listed in all of these periodicals.

Adult Education. Adult Education Assoc. of the U. S. of Amer. 19–27 N. Jackson St., Danville, Ill. ("Professional Literature")

Advertising Agency, and Advertising and Selling. Moore Pub. Co., Inc., 48 W. 38th St., N. Y. 18, N. Y. ("Agency Bookshelf")

American Business. Dartnell Pub., 4660 Ravenswood Ave., Chicago 40, Ill. ("Business Tips")

The American City. Amer. City Mag. Corp., 470 Fourth Ave., N. Y. 16, N. Y. ("Manufacturers catalogs — Get what you want — no charge"; "Municipal and Civic Publications")

The American Economic Review. Amer. Econ. Assoc., Stanford Univ., Stanford, Calif. ("Titles of New Books." Includes pamphlets and documents)

The American Historical Review, A Quarterly. The Macmillan Co., 60 Fifth Ave., N. Y. ("Books Received")

American Journal of Public Health. Amer. Pub. Health Assoc., Inc., 1790 Broadway, N. Y. 19, N. Y. ("Books and Reports")

The American Journal of Sociology. Univ. of
Chicago Press, 5750 Ellis Ave., Chicago 37, Ill.
("Current Books")

Automotive Industries. Chilton Co., Chestnut &
56th Sts., Philadelphia 39, Pa. ("Free Literature")

The Booklist. American Library Association, 50
E. Huron St., Chicago 11, Illinois. ("Free and
Inexpensive Material"; "Free and Inexpensive
Material for Children")

California, Magazine of the Pacific. Calif. State
Chamber of Commerce, 350 Bush St., San Francisco 4, Calif. ("Books." Includes pamphlets)

Changing Times, The Kiplinger Magazine. 1729
H St., Wash. 6, D. C. ("Things to Write for")

Childhood Education. Assoc. for Childhood Educ.
International, 1200 15th St., N. W., Wash. 5, D. C.
("Bulletins and Pamphlets")

Craftsman's World. Amer. Craftsman's Coop-
Council, Inc., 32 E. 52d St., N. Y. 22, N. Y.
("The Bookshelf." Includes Pamphlets)

Distribution Age. Chilton Co., Chestnut & 56th
Sts., Philadelphia 39, Pa. ("Free Literature")

The Education Digest. Ann Arbor, Mich. ("New
Educational Materials")

The Elementary School Journal. Univ. of Chicago
Press, 5750 Ellis Ave., Chicago 37, Ill. ("Publications in Pamphlet Form")

English Journal. 211 W. 68th St., Chicago 21, Ill.
("New Books — Pamphlets")

Factory Management and Maintenance. McGraw-
Hill Pub. Co., Inc., 330 W. 42nd St., N. Y. 36,
N. Y. ("Booklets")

Flow. Flow Magazine, 1240 Ontario St., Cleveland
13, O. ("What's New in Useful Free Literature." Materials, handling and packaging methods)

Foreign Affairs, An American Quarterly Review.
Council on Foreign Relations, 58 E. 68 St., N. Y.
21, N. Y. ("Source Material: II. Pamphlets")

The Instructor. Dansville, N. Y. ("Helpful Teaching Materials for You")

Journal of Home Economics. Amer. Home Econ. Assoc., 1600 20th St., N. W., Wash. 9, D. C. ("From the Editor's Mail")

Library Journal. R. R. Bowker Co., 62 W. 45th St., N. Y. ("You May Want to See")

Management Review. Amer. Management Assoc., 330 W. 42nd St., N. Y. 18, N. Y. ("Briefer Book Notes")

Marriage and Family Living. National Council on Family Relations, 5757 S. Drexel Ave., Menasha, Wisconsin. ("Book Reviews." Includes pamphlets)

Monthly Labor Review. Bureau of Labor Statistics, Wash. D. C. ("Publications of Labor Interest")

The Nation's Schools. 919 N. Michigan Ave., Chicago, Ill. ("The Book Shelf")

The Office. The Office Pub. Co., 270 Madison Ave., N. Y. 16, N. Y. ("New Products." Manufacturer's brochures)

Office Executive. National Office Management Assoc., 132 W. Chilton Ave., Philadelphia 44, Pa. ("Worthy of Reference — Periodicals and Booklets")

Parents Magazine. 85 Newbridge Rd., Bergenfield, N. J. ("Pamphlets for parents"; "Free! Helpful Booklets")

Personnel. Amer. Management Assoc., 330 W. 42nd St., N. Y. 18, N. Y. ("The Personnel Bookshelf")

The Personnel and Guidance Journal. Amer. Personnel and Guidance Assoc., Inc., 20th and Northampton Sts., Easton, Pa. ("Publications . . . in brief")

Practical Home Economics, 351 Fourth Ave., N. Y. 10, N. Y. ("New Teaching Aids." Annual September issue has "Teaching Aids Section," Index of manufacturers offering teaching aids)

Public Administration Review, 1313 E. 60th St., Chicago 37, Ill. ("Reviews of Books and Documents")

Public Health Nursing. Utica, N. Y. ("New Books and other Publications")

Public Management. 1313 E. 60th St., Chicago 37, Ill. ("The Pick of the Month")

Public Personnel Review. Civil Service Assembly, 1313 E. 60th St., Chicago 37, Ill. ("Book Notes." Includes pamphlets)

Public Relations News. 815 Park Ave., N. Y. 21, N. Y. (occasional scattered references)

Publisher's Weekly. (See Listing under 1. Comprehensive Publication Lists)

Quarterly Journal of Economics. Harvard Univ., Cambridge, Mass. ("Recent Publications")

Recreation. National Recreation Assoc., 315 Fourth Ave., N. Y. 10, N. Y. ("Pamphlets")

Rural Sociology. Rural Sociology Society, Univ. of Kentucky, Lexington. ("Current Bulletin Reviews")

Safety Education. 425 N. Michigan Ave., Chicago, 11, Ill. ("Trade Publications")

Sales Management. The Magazine of Marketing. 386 Fourth Ave., N. Y. 16, N. Y. ("Worth Writing For")

School and Society. Society for Advancement of Education, 10 McGovern Ave., Lancaster, Pa. ("Recent Publications")

School Arts. Box 2050, Stanford, Calif. ("Family Circle News Notes"; "The Searchlight")

School Life. Federal Security Agency, Office of Education, Wash. D. C. ("New Books and Pamphlets"; "Educational Aids from your Government"; "Selected Theses on Education")

The School Review. Univ. of Chicago Press, 5750 Ellis Ave., Chicago 37, Ill. ("Educational Writings" — Publications in Pamphlet Form)

Social Forces. Univ. of N. Carolina Press, Chapel

Hill, N. C. ("New Books Received." Includes pamphlets)

Today's Business. B. J. Martin & Co., Chicago 6, Ill. ("Helpful Literature")

Today's Health. 535 N. Dearborn St., Chicago 10, Ill. ("Helpful Hints for Better Living")

Western Advertising. Ramsey Oppenheim Publications, 580 Market St., San Francisco, Calif. ("Books, Booklets")

Wilson Library Bulletin. 950–972 University Ave., N. Y. 52, N. Y. ("Write for These")

IV. FEDERAL AND STATE GOVERNMENT DOCUMENT LISTS

There are countless document lists to use as buying guides, including the separate lists of each government department, Price Lists of many subjects, the Weekly List of Selected U. S. Government Publications, the Monthly Catalog of U. S. Public Documents and the Monthly Checklist of State Publications. These should be checked regularly.

Additional Sources

Boyd, Anne M. and Rose Elizabeth Rips. United States government publications. 3rd rev. ed. N. Y., H. W. Wilson, 1950. 627 p. (Makes clear the coverage of many departments, bureaus, etc. and their publications.)

Melinat, Carl H. Outstanding U. S. government publications of 1951. *Wilson Library Bulletin* 26:829–831, June, 1952. . . . of 1950. *Wilson Library Bulletin* 26:71–73, September, 1951.

"Uncle Sam in the Home." Government publications, 1947–1950. *Booklist* 47:145, December 1, 1950; 47:122, November 15, 1950.

V. BIBLIOGRAPHIES OF PAMPHLETS

Bibliographies of pamphlets are also found in books, magazine articles and pamphlets. Many books of library procedure (such as Fargo, Lyle, and Manley), contain basic lists of pamphlets and documents. Marion Horton's *Buying list of books for small libraries* contains a subject list of pamphlets; Gertrude Forrester's *Occupations* offers a selected list of pamphlets on occupations; the *Standard Catalog for High School Libraries* lists pamphlets under the various subjects, in the main volume as well as supplements. There are many other bibliographies, in book form, of special subjects which list pamphlets; the titles are legion and no attempt will be made to list them.

The following list includes bibliographies of pamphlets in periodical and pamphlet form. It is a beginning list, to which the pamphlet librarian can add many other references. We cannot, however, give a blanket endorsement to all pamphlets listed in all bibliographies.

Agostinelli, Diva.   Sources of information on safety. *Wilson Library Bulletin* 26:843–844, June 1952.
American medical association.   Mimeographed health materials.   The Association, 535 Dearborn St., Chicago 10, Ill.   16 p.
American medical association.   Publications about your health.   The Association, 535 Dearborn St., Chicago 10, Ill.   20 p.
Association of American railroads.   Bibliography of railway literature.   The Association, Transportation bldg., Wash. 6, D. C.   4th ed. 1950.   48 p.
Aviation education, bibliography for elementary schools.   United air lines, School and college service, 80 E. 42nd St., N. Y. 17, N. Y.   12 p.
Aviation education, bibliography for junior and senior high schools.   United air lines, School and college service, 80 E. 42nd St., N. Y. 17, N. Y. rev., March 1947.   16 p.
Aviation education sources, free and low-cost materials.   U. S. Dept. of commerce, Civil aeronautics

administration, Office of aviation development. rev., May 1951. 19 p.

Baker, Alton W., assisted by Franklin S. Rawson. Sources of information on personnel management and labor relations. (Ohio studies in personnel, Research monograph #62.) Bureau of business research, Ohio State university, 1951. 117 p.

Baker library, Graduate school of business administration, Harvard University. House organs. Reference list #8, June 1950. 5 p.

Bennett, Wilma. Occupations filing plan and bibliography of U. S. government publications and other pamphlets on jobs. La Porte, Ind., Powers pub. co., 1951. unpaged.

Beuschlein, Muriel and James M. Sanders. Free and inexpensive teaching aids for the science teacher. *Chicago Schools Journal* Supplement, v. 31, Oct. 1949. Chicago teachers college, 6800 Stewart Ave., Chicago 21, Ill. 32 p.

Boroughs, Homer, Jr., comp. Sources of free and inexpensive instructional materials for northwest teachers. University of Washington press, Seattle 5, Wash. 3d ed., 1951. 46 p.

Branom, Frederick K. Free and inexpensive materials for social studies. *Chicago Schools Journal* Supplement, v. 32, Jan.–Feb. 1951. Chicago teachers college, 6800 Stewart Ave., Chicago 21, Ill. 25 p.

Catalogue of man and nature publications. The American museum of natural history. Central Park West at 79th St., N. Y. 24, N. Y.

Cleveland public library. Business information bureau. *Business information sources.* Bulletin of the Business information bureau. Rose L. Vormelker, The Bureau, Cleveland, Ohio.

Commons, Ellen. Child welfare. Children's bureau pamphlets. *Wilson library bulletin* 27:394, 399, Jan. 1953.

Curriculum bulletin, University of Oregon, Eugene, Oregon. 1951: no. 58 (rev), 59 (rev), 83, 84, 86,

89, 90; 1950: no. 57, 74, 75, 76, 77, 78, 79. Bibliographies of instructional aids to learning.

Fair, Eleanor. Authoritative material on health. *Wilson library bulletin* 22 :400–401, Jan. '48.

Ferguson, Elizabeth. For information on life insurance. *Wilson library bulletin* 23 :200–202, Oct. 1948.

Fornwalt, Russell J. Job getting aids. The Author, Big Brother Movement, 207 Fourth Ave., N. Y. 3. April 1952, 4 p. Oct. 1952, 4 p.

Fornwalt, Russell J. School information sources for educational and vocational counselors. The Author, Big Brother Movement, 207 Fourth Ave., N. Y. 3, N. Y. Nov. 1952, rev. ed. 8 p. mim.

Free and inexpensive learning materials. Division of survey and field services, George Peabody College for Teachers, Nashville, Tenn. 5th ed., 1952. 194 p.

Graham, Earl C. Sources of information on rehabilitation. *Wilson library bulletin* 26 :672–673, April 1952.

Guide to unit material in *The National Geographic Magazine,* 1917–date. Published yearly by Berrien Bindery, Berrien Springs, Michigan. 46 p.

Hall, Elizabeth C. Authoritative material on gardening. *Wilson library bulletin* 22 :726–727, 734, May 1948.

Holland, C., comp. Catalog of free and inexpensive teaching aids for high schools. National association of secondary school principals, Consumer education study, 1201 16th St., N. W., Wash. 6, D. C., 1949.

Jameson, Mary Ethel. Sources of statistical and economic material suitable for a small collection. *Wilson library bulletin* 22 :560–561, March 1948.

Lawrence, Richard M. Sources of information for industrial market research, with special reference to the chemical process industries. *Chemical industries,* 522 Fifth Ave., N. Y. 18, N. Y. 97 p.

Miller, Bruce. Sources of free and inexpensive

teaching aids. The Author, Box 222, Ontario, Calif., 1951. 38 p.

Miller, Bruce. Sources of free pictures. The Author, Box 222, Ontario, Calif., 1951. 27 p.

Myers, Kurtz. Audio-visual bookshelf for busy librarians. Part 1, Audio: *Library journal* 74: 475–477, March 15, 1949; Part 2, Visual: *Library journal* 74:564–568, April 1, 1949.

Myers, Kurtz. The library and audio-visual materials, a bibliography. Audio-visual materials consultation bureau, College of education, Wayne University, Detroit, Mich., 1949. 24 p.

National committee on policies in conservation education. Some selected references on conservation for pupils and teachers. The Committee, 1409 Garfield St., Laramie, Wyoming, 1949. 4 p.

National recreation association. Bibliographies. (on Arts and crafts, Choric speaking, Music, Social recreation, etc.) The Association, 315 Fourth Ave., N. Y. 10, N. Y.

National society for crippled children. Bibliographies. (on Rehabilitation, Special education, Handicapped problems) The Society, 11 S. LaSalle St., Chicago 3, Ill.

Otto, Margaret M. Juvenile delinquency: a pamphlet list. *Wilson library bulletin* 23:384–391, Jan. 1949.

Pangborn, Mark White. The earth for the layman. Selected books and pamphlets (mostly non-technical) on geology, mining, rocks, minerals and gems, fossils, evolution and related subjects. American geological institute, and agency of the National research council, 2101 Constitution Ave., N. W., Wash. 25, D. C. Prelim. ed., Report #2, June 1950. 50 p.

Progress in scientific management, a complete catalog of AMA publications in 8 fields of management, Feb. 1932–Jan. 1952. American Management association, Room 906, 330 W. 42nd St., N. Y., N. Y.

Rankin, Rebecca B. Source materials in public administration. *Wilson library bulletin* 23:732–733, May 1949.

Schofield, Edward T. Bibliographies and sources of audio-visual materials. *Audio-visual guide* 15:5–7, Jan. 1949.

Schwartz, Eleanor E. "Something for nothing." Dept. of libraries, Visual aids and radio board of education, Newark, N. J., Sept. 1950. 56 p.

Selected references for family economics and home management. Prepared by the family-economics home management division of the American home economics association. June 1951. 8 p.

Some sources of free or inexpensive teaching materials on Latin America. Organization of American states, Pan American union, 19th St. & Constitution Ave., Wash. 6, D. C.

Teaching aids, 1952–1953. School service, Westinghouse electric corporation, 401 Liberty Ave., P. O. Box 2278, Pittsburg 30, Pa. 19 p.

U. S. Office of education. Public affairs pamphlets; an index to inexpensive pamphlets on social, economic, political, and international affairs. (Bulletin 1937, no. 3.) Supt. of documents, Wash. D. C., 1937. 85 p. Supplements.

U. S. Office of education. Sources of visual aids for vocational and technical schools. (Pamphlet #80) Supt. of documents, Wash. D. C., 1941.

Willging, Eugene P. The Index to Catholic pamphlets in the English language. Catholic university press, 620–DM Michigan Ave., N. E., Wash. 17, D. C. v. 1, 1937 (o.p.); v. 2, 1942; v. 3, 1946; v. 4, 5, 1948–1950.

Yocum, James C. assisted by Marjorie Landaker. Information sources for small businesses. (Ohio small business handbook, no. B–3, 3d ed., rev.) Bureau of business research, Ohio State university, 1949. 94 p.

3.   PROPAGANDA

One of the most important considerations, if not *the most important,* in the selection of pamphlets is the ability of the librarian to recognize propaganda.   Today's propaganda is not the blatant, crudely-headlined pamphlet printed on cheap paper that it was yesterday; instead it is attractively prepared, well-illustrated and issued by firms that publish 90% harmless pamphlets to gain public good-will and trust. They "slip in" 10% propaganda and therefore it is not recognized.

As other librarians, we, too were unable to detect propaganda and so consulted professional advice (*see* FORE-WORD) before writing this section.   We have read the recommended literature, scanned the "un-American activities" reports, and tried to understand.   When one librarian (in charge of her library's pamphlet collection) talked to us recently about the subject, we told her just what we tell you here: READ AND LEARN, consult your congressmen and send for free state and government literature on un-American investigations.

While librarians have always guarded their "intellectual freedom" very carefully, nevertheless they should ask themselves aren't "reliability of facts" and "intellectual value" also important for libraries to consider?   Isn't freedom a relative matter?   Doesn't society restrict the freedom of a criminal when he violates its code?

An excellent article in the *American Legion Magazine* [2] makes the point clear: "In the library of a middlewestern state university, communist publications — pure propaganda, of no intellectual value — were prominently displayed as if they were reliable data.   Would the equally fantastic "literature" of the Ku Klux Klan have been so displayed?   Consider the intellectual worth of such statements as these: "That the Americans have committed this new crime is an established fact.   Every day brings fresh reports of . . . American planes scattering insects, food . . . infected with disease germs.   Plague, cholera, typhus have been enlisted as

---

[2] The propaganda program of Our Academic. *American Legion Magazine* V. 52: 56, December 1952

allies by the Americans." Or: "The Volunteers soon began to feel that many of the G. I.'s were cowards and inhuman. The cowardice at least could be understood, for the Americans were the hated invaders of a tiny nation thousands of miles from the U. S. with no cause or ideal to inspire them to fight bravely." . . . So the American Communists, from New York City, spoke to students for whom their fellow Americans were fighting and dying, and the library thought it intellectually sound! . . . my point is that our colleges *should know what is being done* by the hidden enemy, should watch the manipulation of the Left Hand."

Some years ago, just previous to World War II, one librarian warned other librarians of the dangers of propaganda. His words are just as good today, altho the propaganda of today is of slightly different nature:[3] "For those of us who have much to do with vertical files that are really used — and that applies to college, school, and public libraries equally — we cannot help but realize how important this matter of propaganda is in the realm of pamphlets, since pamphlets are doubtless the most forceful medium of expression for the person or group with an axe to grind or with a program to promulgate. In short, pamphlets seem to have been especially created for the doctrinaire who must answer that basic human urge to "put it in print and pass it around."

"Thus, the messages of advice in the matter of being vigilant in presenting both sides of every controversial issue must be taken to heart by the vertical file librarian even more seriously than by the librarian who selects the books for the main collection.

"However, although we assume that the reference librarian need never be at a loss to know how to maintain his pamphlet file according to the highest standards, is it possible to say that the problem thus comes to an end? . . . Does the reference file in your own library represent a consistent policy of careful selection, REGULAR weeding, and discriminate balance in all subjects? Were we to take a census today, how many pamphlet files would fall short of the marks set for them?

---

[3] Esterquest, Ralph T. *op. cit.*, p. 226

"Even though the reference librarian maintains a regular policy of checking one or two of the current bibliographies, still the bulk, perhaps 90 per cent, of the contents of his file will usually be made up of unsolicited gift pamphlets from "interest" organizations. Day after day the flood of gifts arrives.

"A word of warning to the reader in passing out the controversial folder should take care of the situation," he concludes,[4] Or would it not be even safer to insert a conspicuous note in these "hot" folders with some message like this:

PLEASE NOTE

"The contents of this folder consist largely of unsolicited literature sent to the library free of charge. For this reason it is likely that a large proportion of the pamphlets are written and distributed by organizations having a more than ordinary interest in the subject, one way or the other. The user of this folder is reminded, therefore, to be on the alert for partisan, biased, and misleading information."

Controversial Subjects

What pamphlet subjects are most likely to be controversial, and which folders should be thus marked? The librarian would do well to read and digest J. Edgar Hoover's "Double Talk Dictionary"[5] which first appeared in 1950 and has since been reprinted, and then watch for the words and phrases which the Communists use and misuse, such as peace, justice, democracy, etc. Controversial subjects may also be found in debate manuals, and the librarian should certainly cover both sides of every debatable, modern question such as Taft-Hartley Act, 1947, World Federation, etc.

Here are some "social problem headings" under which propaganda might appear, since "bigotry" is often disguised in pamphlets as the white man's lack of "brotherhood" and

---

[4] Ibid, p. 227
[5] Hoover, J. Edgar. Double talk dictionary. *Cosmopolitan Magazine* 129: 44, November 1950

"tolerance," and these subjects are typical of those subjects which are often misused to inflame class warfare and religious feeling: Anti-Semitism, Brotherhood of Man, Catholicism, Censorship, Civil Rights, Discrimination, Free Speech, Freedom of the Press, Genocide, Human Relations, Indians, Jews, Minorities, Negroes, Race problems, Social Action, Tolerance, Zionism.

The social science pamphlets are especially prone to contain material of this nature, the experts tell us, and should be carefully screened. Textbooks, novels and other works covering social science subjects have been cited by many investigating committees, and the authors of these books are often found writing pamphlets. Names of these authors and the organizations they represent may be found in state and national reports available free from your congressmen, so the librarian has no excuse for ignorance. An example of such a report is the excellent Fourth Report, Un-American Activities in California, entitled Communist Front Organizations,[5a] which is invaluable to the conscientious librarian who wants to understand propaganda.

Education

Pamphlets on controversial educational subjects should also be carefully considered lest the librarian include and display one-sided material, or overemphasize such controversy. A few of the subjects which are likely to be misused include: Academic freedom, Intercultural education, Loyalty oaths, Progressive education, UNESCO, Workshops, Youth.

One librarian of a large university library was recently questioned by the California Senate Investigating Committee on Education, regarding a display of controversial educational material on the university library bulletin board. A full report of the incident may be read in the 10th Report of the Committee.[6] All pamphlet librarians would be wise

---

[5a] California Legislature. Fourth Report of the Senate Fact-Finding Committee on un-American Activities, 1948. Communist Front Organizations. Sacramento, Calif., 1948. 448 p.

[6] Tenth Report, Senate Investigating Comm. on Educa., The 1951 Sacramento Hearings, Part II, pp. 61–72. Senate of the State of Calif., 1951.

if they studied this Report on Education, as well as the other 9 Reports,[7] available free of charge.

Lists of associations that issue slanted material, not only in California, but throughout the U. S., will be found in these reports, and they are invaluable to the librarian who hopelessly cries: "How can I distinguish 'educational' propaganda? The terminology is so confusing." As the traffic court officer tells you when you pay your fine: "Ignorance of the law is no excuse." READ AND LEARN.

Economics and Politics

Economics and politics come in for a king-size share of propaganda, and usually this type is the easiest to recognize, but not always. Sometimes the pamphlets propagandize by omission. For instance, one pamphlet told of the aggressive expansion policies of the various countries through the ages: United States, Great Britain, Germany and many others were included, but never a word about Russia! Here is a sampling of subjects which should be watched: Capitalism, Collectivism, Communism, Conscientious objectors, Fascism, Immigration and emigration, International relations, International cooperation, Labor, Migratory workers, Peace, Russia, Socialism, Taft-Hartley Act, 1947, World Federation.

Political pamphlets are the subject of a good article written during the war by two librarians:[8] "The pamphleteer has always altered the design of his wares to suit the issues of the times. Among the latter have been economic maladjustment; religious liberty; and slavery with its noncomitant economic and moral aspects. The subject categories of education; labor; philosophy; and socialism have also been invaded. Moreover the political pamphlet serves frequently a dual purpose — to proclaim the attributes of one cause, and to denounce all others as vicious evils. Characteristic, too, are its anonymity; emotional intensity; brevity; cheapness; and simplicity of liter-

---

[7] Reports 1 through 9, Senate Investigating Comm. on Educ., Hearings. Senate of the State of Calif., Sacramento.
[8] Nuremberger, G. A., and Alfred Apsler. Political pamphlets in a university library. *Wilson Library Bulletin* 16: 645, April 1942.

ary form.   And in the pamphlet collection under consideration, if the difference is only in the mode of transmission,
the printed texts of radio broadcasts are identified as political pamphlets."

Summary

A good summary of the dangers of propaganda in the
pamphlet file and the need for alertness is given in an
article in a recent *Wilson Library Bulletin:* [9] "Often those
who will not take time to read books will read brief pamphlets.   This type of reading can be very dangerous if all of
it is of biased nature.   No one will deny that the battle for
the control of our thinking goes on constantly, especially in
these times.   Here the librarian may play an important role
in keeping balance in the pamphlet collection.

"The librarian must be ever on the alert in regard to all
the free material with which libraries are flooded these
days.   Nearly all of it is published to promote the interests
of the organization that issues it . . .

"We all know what happens when the youth of a country
can be indoctrinated with knowledge slanted in one direction.

"Librarians must ever be alert to the need of keeping
material in the pamphlet file balanced.   This means that
student help cannot be used in selecting the items to be
included.   Care must be exercised in ordering, or, in the
case of free material, in selecting the items to be included in
the file.   A fine practice advocated by some librarians is to
include on folders of certain subjects, if folders are used, a
notation that the reader should watch for bias in the presen-
tation of material.   If folders are not used, the librarian
should form the habit of counseling students to watch for
bias and should be ready to give materials on both sides of a
question."

---

9 Schneider, Josephine May.   A pamphlet file in the school and college
library.   *Wilson Library Bulletin* 25: 685, May 1951.

CHAPTER II

Clippings

What and how many newspapers to clip depends entirely upon the individual library. The probable use of such clippings, together with the time and assistance available for the task are the determinants of the situation.

1. LOCAL FILE ESSENTIAL

The chief purpose of newspaper clippings is to preserve local material of current or lasting interest. In the opinion of the writer the first choice of a newspaper to be clipped, therefore, is the best local newspaper. Material pertaining to city, county and state will be useful in any library, and thus every library should have some sort of local file, no matter how small.

The library which has greater need of clippings and has the time and personnel available for this work may choose to clip several papers, as well as some duplicate magazines. The *Christian Science Monitor* is a good second-choice because of the excellence of its general articles, many of which are of permanent value. Another choice would be a newspaper published at the state capital, which would contribute essential facts pertaining to state legislation, etc. We do not recommend clipping the *New York Times,* however, because of its comprehensive index.

Too much clipping of newspapers should be avoided, however. "Clippings should be collected discreetly." That is, they should supplement books and pamphlets rather than substitute for them." says one writer.[1] "The reasons for this being that clippings are apt to be less authoritative than books and though clippings cost less in money, they cost much in time required for gathering, sorting and preparing them for use."

In clipping local material, biographical and historical

---

[1] Brady, Margaret E. Care of fugitive materials. *Wilson Library Bulletin* 26: 259, November 1951

articles are of primary value because this sort of supplementary information is always usable and not likely to be duplicated. A file of current clubs and officers should be maintained, but sometimes this is better kept on cards at the reference desk. A careful check of SUBDIVISIONS FOR LOCAL MATERIAL, in *Supplement I,* will reveal the sort of information that should be clipped. Sunday supplements and special annual issues of local papers often contain invaluable descriptive material. We know of one large library that maintains a file containing not only historical information about its own city and county but about surrounding cities and counties as well. This library believes that the small community libraries do not have adequate staffs to build up such a library for themselves, and that some central collection is needed.

2. MAGAZINES

One must exercise discrimination in clipping magazines, perhaps even more so than in newspapers, as it is a temptation to clip too much because of the attractiveness of the articles, illustrations, etc. The chief rule to remember is: *clip only the subjects which indexes will not locate, or material for which there is a great demand.* To this we make one exception: material of a temporary nature can be clipped to satisfy a temporary demand and later can be discarded.

Small libraries, however, that cannot afford to spend much money for pamphlets and have few indexes would do well to clear out their space-taking files of unbound magazines and clip duplicates and others they do not intend to bind. Almost any magazine that is worth keeping has at least a few articles of reference value. Articles on a similar subject can be stapled together, if necessary, if each is properly marked (see *Marking,* below). In clipping magazines, it is often expedient to clip certain sections such as "What's New in Medicine," "Science," etc. as material for students' themes and outside reading. Material suitable for club programs and holidays is in constant demand. Hobbies are always worth saving; jokes and cartoons should be clipped sparingly.

There are many magazines good for clipping, and such clipping should be done in connection with the Picture File, also. In *addition* to the fifty-three periodicals recommended for clipping pictures, as listed in our *Picture File,*[2] there are many others suitable for the pamphlet file, including the following which cover many subjects:

American Magazine (hobbies, general interest)
Better Homes and Gardens (home and garden, holidays)
Coronet (general interest, photography)
Ford Times (travel, inns)
News-Week (biography, science, temporary current events)
Parent's Magazine (children, holidays, entertaining)
Reader's Digest (general articles, special departments)
Saturday Review of Literature (biography, literature, cartoons)
Sunset (travel, western horticulture)
Time (biography, science, temporary current events)

Sample copies of magazines are also worth examination with the information file in mind. This is especially true of house organs and other trade magazines which often contain a wealth of unindexed material. Take a second glance at that sample before you toss it into the wastebasket!

3. MARKING

The librarian who has charge of the pamphlet file should direct the marking of newspapers and magazines for clipping because it is she who is most familiar with the subjects needed and policies of selection. In the case of newspapers, each page must be scanned and then the articles selected should be marked with brackets at the top by means of a colored pencil. At the top of the front page, the list of pages marked, e.g. pp. 1, 3, 5, 30 should be listed, for the convenience of the person who clips the articles.

When marking magazines, the contents should be rapidly

---

2 Ireland, Norma Olin. The Picture File in School, College and Public Libraries. F. W. Faxon, 1952. p 1, 2.

scanned and important articles wanted should be indicated by paper clips.

4. CUTTING

A page or junior assistant may be trained to do the cutting and will need only be instructed on a few points. Before cutting an article, the date, page and source should be penciled in at the top of the beginning column. Continued articles should be carefully followed and fastened together with paper clips, to be stapled later. It is scarcely necessary to state that all cutting should be neat and straight. After a magazine or newspaper is clipped, the numbers on the front sheet should be scratched and the remainder of the issue immediately destroyed.

5. MOUNTING

"To mount or not to mount" often puzzles the librarian. Our recommendation is to mount all newspaper clippings that are of historical value or will be greatly used; staple together and put into folders all magazine clippings which are too large or lengthy to mount; use envelopes for clippings of temporary or unproved value.

"Until you have learned by experience," one librarian agrees with our last point,[3] "that a particular type of clipping will be subject to heavy demand, it is unwise to take the time for mounting. Insertion in an envelope or folder will do. Manila envelopes that have come through the mail with magazines or pamphlets are very satisfactory for this purpose. Clippings should be grouped according to subject before being put into the envelopes, which have been plainly marked . . ."

Clippings should be mounted on a good grade of paper, but not necessarily a heavy grade; good onion-skin may be used. It has been proved that cheap paper is not satisfactory, especially for clippings that are to be kept permanently. It cracks and falls apart and thus is not recommended. The mounting should be carefully done, leaving some space at the top, especially the upper left-hand corner for the subject heading. Usually four column-widths of newspaper

---

[3] Brady, *op. cit.*, p. 259

may be mounted on one page. Long articles may be mounted on several sheets and then the sheets fastened together with a staple. For labeling clippings, follow the same routine outlined for regular pamphlets as outlined in CHAPTER II, *PAMPHLET HEADINGS*.

6. SUMMARY

Thus, to summarize the procedure for the inclusion of clippings in the pamphlet file, may we say simply this: build up a good local file first, and then clip a few periodicals if you have the time and your file needs the material. Be consistent in your routine and you will eventually have a worthwhile, usable supplementary collection of clippings of permanent value in your pamphlet file.

CHAPTER III

Pamphlet Headings

Pamphlets and clippings should be treated in a similar manner and placed in a common file. A separate file of clippings would be awkward to use and is entirely unnecessary. Therefore the rules and directions regarding stamping, headings, etc., apply to both pamphlets and clippings.

1. MECHANICS

For convenience in placing headings on pamphlets, the use of rubber stamps is recommended. A library can have several made for a nominal sum and they help a great deal in the process. There are many variations of the pamphlet collection stamp which are equally suitable, as follows:

1. V. F. _____
2. PAM _____
3. INF. FILE _____

A date stamp is a necessity in pamphlet processing, in order to date the receipt of pamphlets which is an important factor in revising or weeding the file.

The pamphlet stamp is imprinted horizontally in the upper left hand corner of the pamphlet, allowing sufficient space for the heading to be written, but the date stamp is usually made vertically along the left edge of the pamphlet.

The heading should be lettered in pencil, rather than in ink, because many times it is necessary to change headings after their use has shown a new interpretation, or a further subdivision becomes advantageous.

2. GENERAL RULES

Pamphlet headings should be very simple. Very few subdivisions are necessary, and in most cases they should be avoided. The pamphlet should be studied and scanned carefully, because pamphlet titles are often deceptive. The best probable use of the pamphlet must be considered and this

25

factor should determine the best heading. Heading must be consistent and uniform. *Never* put duplicate copies of the same pamphlet under different headings, no matter how much you are tempted, and avoid headings that are too similar.

As in the case of a picture file, a card record of pamphlet headings should be kept. This is extra work but is well worth the trouble in the end. In this card record will be placed "see" and "see also" references, which are of course essential in any subject heading work. "See" references are used to show that there is nothing under that subject, but that you should see another reference. Example:

> Porcelain, *see*
> Pottery

The main entry here is Pottery. "See also" references, on the other hand, are used to show that there are other similar subjects or more specific subjects, e.g.:

> Accounting, *see also*
> Cost accounting

Both are main entries in this instance. Sometimes the "see also" reference is a general one, as in this case:

> Diseases, *see also*
> Name of disease, e.g. Diabetes

The entry form should follow standard library procedure of spacing, capitalization, etc. Thus the entire record will be uniform and standardized. However, that does not mean that such a card file cannot include clues to elusive material. As in the case of certain bulletins and numbered proceedings, etc. (see CHAPTER IV, on *CATALOGS AND REPORTS*) a location record is important and this may well be incorporated in the subject heading file. The librarian should use cross-references generously, in order that a complete index of the pamphlet file is available on cards.

3. SPECIAL PROBLEMS

Headings and cross-references for local material (state, county and city) present the largest problem in pamphlet headings. A list of SUBDIVISIONS FOR LOCAL MATERIAL: CITY, COUNTY AND STATE will be found in *Supplement I*. There should be three separate groups of headings (with appropriate subdivisions) for the state, county and city in which your library is located. Put *all* material pertaining to these places directly under the local heading, rather than under the subject. It was our task, a few years ago, to accept a position in a library for the express purpose of revising that library's pamphlet file. We found hundreds of good local pamphlets buried under general subjects, and our first work was assembling these together under the appropriate headings for their city, county and state. It was amazing how useful this change immediately proved, and the circulation of such pamphlets increased almost 100%. Sometimes it seems rather difficult to do, as it differs from the usual catalog practice, but the usefulness of such a file proves its worth.

For instance, put pamphlets under *California — Taxation,* rather than *Taxation — California*. From your subject heading Taxation, then, make a cross-reference card in your subject heading file, as follows:

Taxation, *see also*
California — Taxation

The same procedure applies to county and city pamphlets. Sometimes it seems like a duplication of effort and unnecessary work to make so many cross-references, but remember you are not the only user of the file, therefore you must make it "fool-proof."

4. INCLUSIONS AND EXCLUSIONS

This edition of our "Pamphlet File" contains some differences from the early edition. Experience with various pamphlet collections has shown us that certain new inclusions should be made, as well as certain exclusions.

In the first place, we have excluded all names of organizations, corporations, etc. as subject headings, with a very few exceptions, such as American Red Cross. Since most of these organizations were originally listed because of their reports or historical summaries received (no general subjects under these headings), we felt that such listing was really not essential in our list of headings, as each library would vary according to the reports received in that library. Many of these organizations are included in our PARTIAL LIST OF ORGANIZATIONS, ETC. THAT ISSUE PAMPHLETS, in *Supplement II.*

Geographical headings are included in our new list of pamphlet headings, for the convenience of the librarian. Formerly we had listed them only in our *Picture File* [1] but had not included them with the pamphlets because we thought it a duplication of effort. But since not all libraries maintain a picture collection and are thus unfamiliar with the geographical headings used, we decided to include them in this edition of *The Pamphlet File,* for the convenience of the pamphlet librarian. We have consulted the latest atlases for names of new states and geographical divisions, and have endeavored to include the majority of countries, islands, etc., but we make no claim for absolute completeness.

We have excluded most of the form subdivisions found in our earlier work, although sometimes included a few which we thought of sufficient importance to that particular subject. Form divisions which we have largely excluded in this edition are: Description and travel, Economic conditions, Finance, History, Politics and government, Social life and customs, Study and Teaching, etc.

5. NEW HEADINGS

In addition to the various changes in headings mentioned, we have included many headings which are entirely new, subjects that have assumed new importance in the last few years, as well as distinctly new topics. We cannot take the space to list these headings but here are a few samples of the new headings taken from the "A" section of our LIST OF PAMPHLET HEADINGS.

ACTH (Hormone)
Airplanes — Jet propelled

---

[1] Ireland, Norma Olin. The Picture File in School, College, and Public Libraries. Boston, F. W. Faxon Co., 1952

Allergy
Amino acids
Antibiotics
Aureomycin

As stated in the FOREWORD, we have over 2,000 subject headings in our new work, as compared to 1468 in the earlier edition. And no doubt you will add many more new ones, as you expand your pamphlet file along with the times.

6. OTHER SOURCES FOR HEADINGS

Since our *Pamphlet File* makes no claim for absolute completeness, but is intended, rather, for the medium-sized school, college and public library, we are glad to recommend other sources for subject headings:

I. PERIODICAL INDEXES

Reader's Guide for most general headings, but Industrial Arts, P.A.I.S., Education Index, Art Index are likewise adaptable. New York Times good for *very* new material, not yet found in magazines.

II. GENERAL SUBJECT HEADING "LISTS"

Sears and Monroe's *List of Subject headings for small libraries,* along with the large and complete Library of Congress and A.L.A. Lists, may be used as a supplementary tool. Ball's *Subject headings for the information file* is pertinent, and for children's pamphlets, the librarian may employ Smith's *Subject headings for children's books.*
Special Library Association's Classification committee has collected *Classification schemes and subject heading lists,* loan collection, compiled by Isabel L. Towner. This is a general list to be used in connection with the Special Subject Heading "Lists" noted in the next section.

III. SPECIAL SUBJECT HEADING "LISTS"

While the following list is highly specialized, nevertheless the books listed may be referred to when special collections of pamphlets are acquired or when special subjects pamphlets are difficult to classify. This list should be useful to college and university libraries, special libraries, and large, departmentalized public libraries.

Aeronautics

Gautreaux, Agnes Angèle. Aviation subject headings. N. Y., Special libraries assoc., 1949. 56 p.

Special libraries assoc. Engineering-aeronautics section. Subject headings for aeronautical engineering libraries. N.Y., Special libraries assoc., 1949. 245 p.

U. S. Library of Congress. Division of aeronautics. Subject headings for the aeronautical index . . . Division of aeronautics, Library of Congress. N.Y., 1940. 106 p.

Chemistry

Special libraries assoc. Chemistry section. A list of subject headings for chemistry libraries. N. Y. Special libraries assoc., 1945. 53 p.

Cities and Towns

U. S. National resources commission. Classified guide to material in the Library of Congress covering urban community development. Wash. D. C., The Comm., 1936. 102 p.

Civil Service

U. S. Civil Service commission. The arrangement of public administration materials. Wash., D.C., The Library, U. S. civil service commission, 1945. 120 p.

Education

Pettus, Clyde Elaine. Subject headings in education; a systematic list for use in a dictionary catalog. N.Y., H. W. Wilson Co., 1938. 188 p.

Voegelein, Lily Belle. List of educational subject headings. Columbus, The Ohio State university press, 1928. 337 p.

Finance

Special libraries assoc. Financial group. Banking and financial subject headings for bank libraries and financial information files . . . N. Y., Special libraries assoc., 1940. 98 p.

Language and Literature

U. S. Library of Congress. Catalog division. Literature subject headings with list of Shakespeare collections and language subject headings. 5th ed. Wash., D.C., Library of Congress, 1926. 147 p.

Law

U. S. Library of Congress. Law library. Tentative headings and cross-references for a subject catalogue of American and English law . . . Wash., D.C., Govt. print. off., 1911. 150 p.

Music

Music library association. Subject headings for the literature of music . . . mim. for the Music library assoc., Rochester, 1935. 37 p.

Ohman, Hazel Eleanor. A music subject heading system. N.Y., The Author, 1932. 24 p.

U. S. Library of Congress. Subject catalog division. Music subject headings used on printed catalog cards of the Library of Congress. Wash., D.C., Govt. print. off., 1952. 133 p.

Names, Geographical

U. S. Library of Congress. Subject catalog division. Period subdivisions under names of places used in the dictionary catalogs of the Library of Congress. Wash., D.C., Govt. print. off., 1950. 75 p.

Negroes

Yocum, F. L. A list of subject headings for books by and about the negro. N.Y., H. W. Wilson Co., 1940. 35 p.

Nursing

National league of nursing education. Curriculum committee. A library handbook for schools of nursing. . . . N.Y., The League, 1936. 264 p. Pt. II — List of subject headings.

Occupations

Bennett, Wilma. Occupations filing plan and bibliography of U. S. government publications and other pamphlets on jobs. La Porte, Indiana, Powers publishing co., 1951. unp.

Harness, Robert B. Subject headings for pamphlets in an occupational vertical file. (Information circular #111, Feb., 1951). Univ. of Illinois library, Chicago undergraduate division, Chicago 11, Ill., 1951. 16 p. mim.

Physics

Voigt, Melvin John. Subject headings in physics. Chicago, American library association, 1944. 151 p.

Public administration

U. S. Civil service commission. The arrangement of public administration materials. Wash., D.C., Library, U. S. Civil service commission, 1945. 120 p.

Religion

Kapsner, Oliver Leonard, father. Catholic subject headings . . . Collegeville, Minn., St. John's Abbey press, 1942. 426 p. First supplement, 1943. 59 p.

Pettee, Julia. List of theological subject headings and corporate church names based upon the headings in the catalogue . . . Chicago, American library assoc., 1947. 653 p.

Science. See Technology

Social Work

Social welfare: a list of subject headings in social work and public welfare. N.Y., Special libraries assoc., 1937. 64 p.

Sociology

A London bibliography of the social sciences . . . London, London school of economics and political science, 1931–1932. 4 v. (v. 4 includes subject headings)

Technology

Pittsburgh. Carnegie library. Index to subject catalogue of the Technology department. Pittsburgh, Carnegie library, 1909. 50 p.

War

British museum. Department of printed books. Subject Index of the books relating to the European war, 1914–1918 . . . London, Printed by order of the trustees, 1922. 196 p.

Special libraries association. War subject headings for information files. N.Y., Special libraries assoc., 1942. 56 p.

CHAPTER IV

Weeding: Catalogs and Reports

The process of weeding means, of course, the discarding of pamphlets that are no longer useful because they are out-of-date, no longer needed, or replaced by better material in books. The vertical file should be overhauled thoroughly at least once a year, oftener if possible.

1. REVISION

It is our opinion that weeding should be a continuous process, or perhaps we should call in "revision." Whenever new pamphlets are added to the file, it would be well if the librarian would glance through the pamphlets on the same subject, and discard those pamphlets which are replaced by the newer, better material. We have discussed balance of material in CHAPTER I, *SELECTION,* as well as propaganda, so we shall not elaborate on this phase of the subject. But alertness in careful weeding is a necessary quality for the pamphlet librarian. "It should not be assigned to student assistants," [1] says one college librarian about weeding, "for only persons trained in handling the collection and in working with the students and faculty would know how best to weed a collection. When it is impossible to find time to check the whole collection even once a year, the librarian or one of the assistant librarians should weed at least those parts of it that seem particularly crowded. Collections of state and local material should be kept intact because of the special value of such material for state and local history.

"Other fields which should not be discarded are those in which the book collection is weak, those needed by faculty members for the reserve shelf from time to time, and items not to be found elsewhere. Otherwise the collection should be pruned severely and as often as time permits. A record

---

[1] Schneider, Josephine May. The pamphlet file in the school and college library. *Wilson Library Bulletin* 25: 687, May 1951.

should be kept of the number of pamphlets discarded so
that at all times an estimate of the total holdings is available.
In our library discarded pamphlets are so marked and are
put on a rack of materials free to students."

2. CATALOGS AND REPORTS

A definite policy should be decided upon and maintained,
in the case of catalogs and reports. Shall they be included
in the pamphlet file, and if so how long shall they be kept,
are questions to be answered. In the case of college catalogs, we suggest that you exclude them, unless the library
receives less than half a dozen per year. They are bulky
and soon fill up a vertical file. It is recommended that they
be shelved in alphabetical order by name of college, on regular bookshelves.

In the case of publishers' catalogs, with certain exceptions
they are usually kept in the order department, so therefore
they present no problem. In regard to other forms of catalogs, such as seed catalogs, etc., the library must make its
own decision according to space available and demand for
such material.

Reports constitute another problem. Here the question
of cataloging enters in, which presents a new factor to be
considered. Shall reports be treated as books and be cataloged as continuations, shall they be shelved with periodicals,
or kept in the vertical file with pamphlets? Here again it
is a case for the individual library to decide, because any one
or all three of the three methods can be used, depending on
the report or proceeding. Many government document reports are of sufficient value to catalog and of course certain
series are regularly bound. Then there are proceedings of
societies, etc. that are better kept with the periodicals since
they are indexed in periodical indexes.

For annual reports that have current value only or whose
importance has not yet been established, the pamphlet file
is the solution. However, three considerations should be
observed. In the first place, in the case of annual reports
of temporary value, retain only the latest year. In order
to keep up to date, check your mailing list of such societies,
etc. every year, in order that it is active. Secondly, in the

case of bulletins and numbered proceedings, it is wise to keep a special card-record, showing their location in the file. Otherwise they will not easily be located. In the third place, a careful selection policy must be observed in the acceptance of catalogs and reports, as in the case of pamphlets. If you do not wish to include the pamphlets of a certain association or agency, why should you give room to its annual report? A careful checking of all organizations, as suggested in the section on Propaganda, is again emphasized.

CHAPTER V

Storage and Circulation

There are three methods of storing pamphlets — in pamphlet boxes, on regular shelves cataloged as books, and in vertical files or other cabinets. Since the latter is the method most popular in libraries today, we shall consider it first.

1. VERTICAL FILE

Although we consider a vertical file as a wood or steel cabinet, broadly speaking it can include folders or envelopes arranged in an upright position in a box, drawer or tray. Many libraries hesitate to start a pamphlet collection because of lack of financial means to buy a vertical file; they feel that without a standard cabinet such an undertaking would be impossible. This is untrue, however, because orange crates or apple boxes can provide a good beginning for such a collection, especially in a small school library where the needs will necessarily be small.

If a vertical file cabinet is feasible, however, the librarian should know that such files are built for expansion and individual units may be purchased separately. They usually consist of four drawers per unit. There are many styles and types of cabinets available — wood and steel, in both letter and legal size. Some librarians prefer to match their shelves, while others choose for various other reasons.

There are many library furniture-supply houses which will furnish catalogs and prices on such files, including Gaylord, Library Service, Remington-Rand, etc. The Hobart Cabinet Co. of Troy, Ohio, also offers an "Economy Steel Cabinet" consisting of 27 drawers 12" × 9" × 3" each, and several units may be used together. Folders need not be used and it is very reasonably priced. The writer used such a file successfully in one library which did not have a vertical file.

Dictionary Arrangement

A vertical file is suitable for a dictionary arrangement of pamphlets, which method is of course the most easy and convenient for staff and patrons alike. Many libraries assign an arbitrary classification number to pamphlets but still file alphabetically under subjects. In the writer's opinion, classification of pamphlets in the vertical file is a burdensome procedure, entirely unnecessary.

To summarize the advantages of a vertical file, we list the following:

1. Dictionary arrangement, for simple preparation
2. Economy of space
3. Simplicity and convenience of use

Other advantages named by libraries include the ease of filing pamphlets, the elasticity of the system, and the coordination of related material.

Guides and Folders

There are many different kinds of vertical file equipment available, but for our purpose we shall describe only two — guides and folders. We recommend metal-tab guides for the alphabet letter and main subject divisions, and heavy manila folders for the pamphlets. Envelopes are not desirable for pamphlets, as a general rule, because of their inconvenience to use. In choosing pamphlet folders, however, always be sure that they are of excellent quality paper, because otherwise they will crack and deteriorate quickly.

Small pamphlets may be placed upright in double rows in each individual subject folder and large ones horizontally. The latter should all be placed in the same position (reading from left to right), because it makes the file easier to use.

Type of Heading

Headings for folders may be one of two types — either lettered neatly in black ink, or typed on slips (especially provided for that purpose) and pasted onto the folder. Typed headings give the file a neat, professional appearance, while lettered headings are easier and quicker to prepare and to read. It is a matter for the individual library to decide.

Other Storage Methods

Since the purpose of this book is the preparation of pamphlets primarily for a Vertical File, with headings listed for this method, we shall not deal with other methods in detail such as pamphlet boxes. As we have stated in our chapter on WEEDING, certain catalogs and documents have their place in pamphlet boxes. But in recent years the tendency has been for libraries to use the vertical file for the majority of uncataloged pamphlets, and abandon the partial classification of pamphlets and storage in boxes.

The cataloging of certain pamphlets, however, is a real consideration in any work on pamphlet preparation. Pamphlets of permanent value which supplement or fill in lacks of the book collection should certainly be cataloged. They may be placed in special pamphlet board-covers, designed for this purpose, and thus take on the appearance of books. Sometimes a pamphlet that has proven its value in the pamphlet file may be withdrawn and cataloged; we recommend that a duplicate be purchased. The reference librarian could well list such pamphlets and recommend their duplicate purchase to the order librarian.

2. CIRCULATION OF PAMPHLETS

The routine for the circulation of uncataloged pamphlets is very similar to that used for the circulation of books. They are stamped with the date due on the back of the pamphlet and also on the pamphlet card. Permanent cards are like those used for pictures and may be simply labeled according to the card illustrated on page 40.

The cards are not kept with the individual pamphlets, however, but rather are placed at the desk to be used again — one card for each person's charge. For instance, one reader may take out six pamphlets on six different subjects, but they are all recorded on one pamphlet card. The number of pamphlets to be issued to one person and the time limit to be set are matters of individual library procedure. They are decided by the use of the file and the number of pamphlets available.

PAMPHLETS # 1

DATE	BORROWER' NAME & ADDRESS ISSUED TO	NO. & SUBJECT OF PAMS.
4/12/35	Mary Smith	10--
	21 High St.	Cookery

Library Bureau   Cat. No. 1152.6

Other Methods and Short-cuts

The use of charging machines may alter the system of pamphlet circulation and of course many small libraries have worked out their own different methods and short-cuts. One article,[1] written several years ago but still apropos, describes one of these: "For circulation of material from the vertical file, all large envelopes in which periodicals and pamphlets are delivered to the library are kept at the circulating desk. Cards similar to those used for periodicals, except for another color, with the heading "Vertical File" are kept on file at the desk. In the Greenville (S.C.) Public Library, all material, except that marked not to circulate, may be taken from the vertical file for a period of seven days without privilege of renewal. When the reader presents material from the vertical file, a list of the subjects with number of clippings or pamphlets on each subject is made on one of the vertical file cards. The reader is then asked to write his name, library number of both, according to library policy, below the charge. This charge is repeated on one of the brown envelopes, selected to correspond in size with the material being taken, and a circle drawn on the envelope to enclose the charge. The date due is then stamped beside the name of the reader on the vertical file card and within the circle on the envelope in which the material is taken. The reader is cautioned to return the vertical file material in the same envelope and to use the charge on the envelope to check on material being returned. The vertical file cards are held for count and to be filed in the date due file for the corresponding date.

"When the vertical file material is returned to the library, the assistant searches under date due for the vertical file card on which the charge tallies with that on the envelope. If all material is present, the card returns to the file on the desk and the material is routed for filing in the vertical file. Otherwise, the vertical file card, with indication as to what material is still to be returned, goes back into the date due file to await return of other material or to be

---

1 Wofford, Azile. Circulating non-book materials. *Wilson Library Bulletin* 15: 653, 655, April 1941

treated as overdue . . . The methods outlined above are simple, inexpensive and effective."

Identification of Pamphlets

The identification of pamphlets sometimes involves problems, especially when there is some question as to their return. One school librarian tells us how she solves this problem:[2] "We have solved the problem of identification by the simple expedient of assigning a number (like an accession number) to each piece of material that goes into the pamphlet file . . .

"When a borrower takes out several pamphlets with the same subject heading, they are all charged on the same charge card by listing the numbers of the different pamphlets. When the material is returned it is discharged by crossing off the numbers on the charge card which correspond to the numbers on the pamphlets returned. If the pamphlets are not all returned at once, the charge card is put back under the date due until the rest of the material is returned . . . The method has been used here for eight or nine years, and we have found it satisfactory as well as simple."

---

[2] Brue, Dorothy. Has no trouble with circulating ephemeral items. *Library Journal* 76: 732, May 1, 1951

CHAPTER VI

Uses: Publicity

The uses of the pamphlet collection are many and varied. The popularity of certain subjects varies in different types of libraries, according to the patrons of that library. There are certain uses of this material, nevertheless, that may apply to all libraries.

1. GENERAL USES

As we have stated before, the pamphlet file supplements the book collection, making the very latest material available to the library. This is especially important in reference work, where questions are asked daily in which such material is needed. Biographies, holidays, vocations, hobbies, current events, local history — these are only a few of the general subjects requested, for which we may turn to the pamphlet file. Then, too, when there is a "run" on periodical literature for a certain subject of timely interest, the pamphlet file can be used to supplement periodical literature.

School and College Libraries

School and college libraries have similar uses for the pamphlet file, so in this instance they will be discussed together. Although topics assigned to college and high school students differ materially, the general purposes are very much the same. Material for debates, special reports, term papers, etc. may all be supplied from the pamphlet file. One college reference librarian expresses it thus:[1] "In a small college library with a limited number of reference volumes, pamphlets can well supplement the book collection. Summer statistics for 1950 at this library indicate a representative per cent of questions found solution in the pamphlet collection. Popular in appeal and preferred by

---

[1] Powell, A. Scott. The pamphlet population. *Wilson Library Bulletin* 25: 381, January 1951

43

students, pamphlets should not be taken lightly as to resource value to research students and workers."

The librarian should be familiar not only with various courses offered in the curriculum, but also with the different assignments given out, whenever this is possible. In a school library this is a much easier matter than in a college or university library. The present trend in higher education, however, is a far closer cooperation between librarians and professors in regard to knowledge of subjects offered, and assignments. Methods of acquainting the teachers and professors with the pamphlet file will be discussed later under the head of "Publicity."

In the case of school libraries, sometimes departments build up their own separate pamphlet collections. This practice is not recommended, as the central library is the logical place for such a collection. "In a school with a library and librarian," says one librarian,[2] "it makes for efficiency for all departments to turn over to the library such pamphlet material as they want the pupils to use for reference. Many departments overlap in their topics — food pamphlets are of interest to students of domestic science, of chemistry, and of biology. If pamphlets are kept in department libraries there is unnecessary duplication, or material is lacking which might have been available had one department known that the other department had it. It has meant no small sacrifice to the department to give up their treasures to this main collection in the school library, but they themselves have expressed their appreciation for the better organization and methods of the library for keeping track of such ephemeral material when lent to either pupils or teachers."

Public Libraries

It is in the public library that we see the varied uses of the pamphlet collection. Because of the diversity of patrons' interests, including those of professional and business men, homemakers, unemployed, students, and a great many mis-

---

[2] Brady, Margaret E. Care of fugitive materials. *Wilson Library Bulletin* 21: 258, November 1951

cellaneous readers, we have requests for every imaginable subject.

Cookery, beauty hints, budgets and other household problems including child care, interior decoration and consumer buying are only a few of the topics which homemakers may find of interest in the pamphlet file. The government publishes many pamphlets which are not only authoritative, but contain the best material available on these subjects. With the continued interest in consumer buying and education, the family shopper is demanding the best in everything. In order to get the best, she must understand certain standards and specifications, and these should be available in the pamphlet file.

Vocational pamphlets are in constant use not only by the student, but by the veteran. Since the war pamphlets on "Starting your own business" have been increasingly popular with returned G. I.s, and have been worth their weight in gold.

Valuable pamphlets are also available for the businessman and such pamphlets often form the beginning of a business collection. In emphasizing the value of such a collection, including pamphlets, the reference assistant in one public library expressed it thus: [3] "The initial expense and difficulties of setting up a special collection are not as great as might be anticipated. As a foundation there is the "Establishing and Operating" series published by the Foreign and Domestic Commerce Bureau of the U.S. Dept. of Commerce. These pamphlets offer information on organization and management of various types of small business. Each booklet treats location, selection, record keeping, sales methods, financing, display, etc. In all, there are some forty different pamphlets available, none priced higher than eighty-five cents, with most types of retail establishment covered in the series.

"Several excellent booklists and acquisition aids are available from which selectively to acquire a working collection of business books and pamphlets . . . Trade associations . . . and local chambers of commerce provide much free

3 Wasserman, Paul. Are we neglecting the small businessman? *Wilson Library Bulletin* 25: 625, April 1951

and inexpensive material. Examination of their catalogs will uncover much of infinite value and pertinence to the small businessman."

2. PAMPHLET READABILITY

The increasing popularity of pamphlet material opens the door for studies of readability, and at least one survey has been made on the subject. This was a study of eleven pamphlets on home economics sampled by fifty freshman girls majoring in the subject at Ohio State university. The results were published in a recent article in the *Occupations* magazine by the Assistant Jobs Editor of *Charm* magazine. She says:[4] "Most of us have looked through a folder of pamphlets from a library file on occupations and noticed some pamphlets well thumbed and dog-eared, and others, resting in the folder for as many months and covering the same material, that still look new and unused.

"What makes one pamphlet more popular than another? Apparently, subject matter isn't the answer, since all the pamphlets in the folder cover the same ground. Nor is adequacy of coverage a complete answer. Some of the pamphlets are not read even though they provide the best coverage of the subject."

In discussing the actual results of the Survey mentioned, the writer summarizes:[5] "The more popular pamphlet not only had more pictures; it also had more outlining, a less dense-appearing mass of type on the page, and a more "personal" writing style. This would indicate that any appraisal and rating of occupational information pamphlets will probably have to be based on several measures of different aspects of style and format.

"These results also indicate that the appearance of the pamphlet is a more important factor in influencing its popularity than many of us had believed.

"We conclude that . . . the pamphlet that *looked easy to read,* and from which *information could be easily obtained* was the more popular one."

---

4 Oxhandler, Avis. What makes an occupational information pamphlet popular. *Occupations* 29: 26, October 1950
5 Ibid., p. 29

The subject of readability in pamphlets is discussed from another angle, that of writing and publication, in a pamphlet [6] by Crosby issued a few years ago. It is worth the librarian's attention.

3. PUBLICITY

Librarians are constantly working out interesting displays to feature pamphlets on all subjects. Exhibits, with books and pamphlets together, supplemented by posters and pictures, are also widely used. As in the case of the picture file, there is no use in building up a collection of material unless you advertise it effectively to your borrowers. Publicity by means of displays, exhibits, newspaper articles and feature stories are all means to this end.

"Smaller, cheaper than books," [7] says Marie Loiseaux, Editor of *Wilson Library Bulletin* and specialist in public relations, "pamphlets are quicker to write and print, and therefore far easier to keep up to the minute than books. In this scientific age, when minutes make differences in technical data, this is an important factor. Libraries have various ways of making pamphlets available, though generally the public knows and uses them far less than the pamphlets' usefulness — and the readers' needs — merit. Again, the public memory is short; we can never tell them often enough about these helpful, often overlooked aids."

"Attractive, provocative and informative as they are, pamphlets are nevertheless all too often left in their places in public libraries, where their charm and usefulness are hidden behind the bland façade of a filing cabinet," states another librarian.[8] She then describes a twelve-month calendar of exhibits, allowing for fortnightly changes of pamphlet displays: "These are arranged by the use of a simple wooden rack, 16″ high and 48″ long, made by the janitor. It is placed between the main charging desk and the reading room to catch the attention of both incoming

---

6 Crosby, Alexander L. Pamphlets that pull. National Publicity Council for Health and Welfare Services, 1948
7 Loiseaux, Marie D. Talking shop. *Wilson Library Bulletin* 21: 441, February 1947.
8 Taylor, Helene Scherff. Pamphlets on display. *Wilson Library Bulletin* 410, January 1941.

friends and browsing borrowers. Against a background of bright but suitable colored poster paper, even the most anemic pamphlet covers have attracted notice. At the base of the rack a printed sign announces: THESE MAY BE BORROWED FOR ONE WEEK. Across the top, various legends, selected for timeliness, take their turn in luring many an indifferent glance to profitable inspection.

"At the end of a year's trial, the measurable results of this scheme have been so satisfactory that its continuation is taken as a matter of course. Circulation statistics have soared most gratifyingly, far beyond records for previous years. It would seem that once the members of the public have been made conscious of these sources of information, they go directly to the vertical files themselves to augment regular reading matter."

Other Means of Publicity

Another means of publicity, especially suitable for school and college libraries, is the sending of special lists of pamphlets to teachers and professors. Go through your list of subject headings, copying those of special interest to certain departments. Type the list and label it in this manner:

"Subjects Found in the Pamphlet File on _____"

You will find that the teachers will be more than pleased with this information and glad to use it in making assignments. It is an excellent means of cooperation with the teaching staff.

There are various outside sources which may benefit from announcements of your new pamphlets and which in turn will help advertise your collection. "Friends of the Library," Historical societies, Garden clubs, Women's clubs, and Civic organizations of all kinds are excellent sources.

Posters and exhibits in public buildings, store-windows, flower shows, animal shows, fairs, etc. are also recommended. Sometimes library booths may be arranged at fairs, and these can well include new, bright pamphlets.

Within the library, colored backgrounds and interesting captions help to "sell" pamphlets. Sometimes a bright new cover on a pamphlet will help. Call attention to new pamphlets at staff meetings, in order that all librarians become interested. "Catchy" phrases should be used with displays, such as the following:

> "Follow the Seasons with Pamphlets"
> "Good Things Come in Small Packages"
> "Learn and Earn with Pamphlets"
> "For Men Only"
> "Use Your Government"
> "Your City Takes Inventory"
> "Yesterday and Today"
> "Pamphlets for Young Moderns"

Add pamphlets to all bibliographies prepared in the library, include them in booklists whenever possible, and do not forget to mention them on your radio and television programs.

Collateral Reference Guides

Some libraries use collateral reference guides in the card catalog to advertise their pamphlets. They read like this:

For further material on the above subject, consult the SPECIAL COLLECTIONS which are checked below:

(If you cannot find what you want, the librarian will be glad to help you.)

☑ Pamphlet file   ☐ Public documents
☐ Clipping File   ☐ Picture collection
☐ Periodical indexes   ☐ Art collection
☐ Local history collection   ☐ Music collection
☐ Maps   ☐ Lantern slides

They are very useful and unify the book and pamphlet collections. There are certain difficulties to this system, however, which should be fully considered before adopting it. First of all, the subject headings for pamphlets are not always the same as those for books. The former are simpler and have fewer subdivisions. This causes a real difficulty and involves cross-references. Secondly, the system involves the addition of new subject headings to the catalog, many of which are temporary. In the third place, inclusion means that revision and discarding must be kept up accurately, and whenever the pamphlet file has certain subjects weeded out, the corresponding subject cards must be removed. It takes a great deal of time and care, and must be done in close cooperation with the librarian who files cards in the catalog. It is an excellent means of informing the public about the pamphlet file, but a difficult one to administer.

Sign on the Catalog

Just as effective a method, and a much simpler one, is to print a large sign and place it on top of the catalog. You can choose your own wording, but here are two possibilities:

(1)

IF YOU CANNOT FIND
THE SUBJECT YOU WANT IN THE CATALOG
TRY THE **PAMPHLET FILE**
For further help, ask the Reference Librarian

(2)

DO YOU NEED MORE MATERIAL
ON YOUR SUBJECT?
TRY THE **PAMPHLET FILE**
Ask the Reference Librarian about it

4. SUMMARY

In conclusion, we shall say that a pamphlet file is a needed collection in every library, large or small; with careful planning and supervision on the part of the librarian in charge, it may become an extremely valuable asset. Publicity is extremely important in this day and age, and efforts taken to publicize pamphlets are usually most rewarding. The librarian in charge of this collection must be constantly striving to find new uses for pamphlets and new ways to publicize their use. With the librarian's constant alertness in the careful selection of both pamphlets and clippings, combined with diligent arrangement and preparation for the widest use, the importance of the pamphlet collection in school, college and public libraries is unquestionable. And with new and better means of publicity constantly developing, *the future of this media of information is unlimited.*

LIST OF PAMPHLET HEADINGS

A

Abnormal Children.   *See* Children — Abnormal

Abolition of slavery.   *See* Slavery

Abrasives

Abyssinia.   *See* Ethiopia

Academic freedom
See also Loyalty, Oaths of

Accidents
See also Automobile accidents
Prevention of

Accidents, Industrial
See also Workmen's compensation

Accounting
See also Cost accounting

Acoustics

ACTH (Hormone)

Acting
See also Actors and actresses; Amateur theatricals; Drama; Moving picture actors and actresses, Theater; Theater, Little; etc.

Actors and actresses
See also Moving picture actors and actresses

Adjustment
Personal
Vocational

Adolescence
See also Boys; Girls; Youth

Adoption

Adult education
See also Correspondence schools and courses; Opportunity schools; University extension

Advertising
History

Advertising, Art in.   *See* Commercial art

Aerodynamics

Aeronautic research

Aeronautics
See also Airplanes; Airports; Autogiros; Helicopters; etc.
Commercial
Laws and regulations

Afghanistan

Africa
See also Congo, Belgian; Egypt, etc.

Age.   *See* Old Age; Youth

Age and employment
See also Older workers

Age-grade progress

Agricultural administration

Agricultural credit

Agricultural engineering

Agricultural machinery

Agriculture (subdivided by name of country, etc.)
Cooperative
Economic aspects
Farm relief
Finance
History
Vocational

Agriculture, Soilless.   *See* Plants — Soilless culture

Air bases

Air conditioning

Air Force.   *See* United States — Air Force

√ **Air polution**
See also Smoke prevention; Smog

Air raids

Air travel

Air warfare

Air-mail service

Airplane engines

Airplanes
Jet propelled

Airplanes in agriculture

Airports

Airships

Airways

Alabama

Alaska

Albania

Alchemy

Alcohol
Industrial

√ **Alcoholism**
See also Liquor problem; Prohibition

Alfalfa

Algeria

Aliens
See also Chinese in the U. S.; Displaced persons; Immigration and emigration; Italians in the U. S.; Japanese in the U. S.; Naturalization; etc.

All-year schools.   *See* Vacation schools

Allergy

Alloys

Almanacs
See also Calendar

Alphabets
See also Lettering

Aluminum

Amateur theatricals
See also Theater, Little

Amber

Amerasia case

America
Antiquities
Discovery and exploration
History

American colonies.   *See* Colonial life and customs

American Education Week

American Federation of Labor

American Legion

American Library Association
Conferences

American literature
See also Authors

American National Red Cross.   *See* Red Cross

American Samoa

Americanism

Americanization.   *See* Naturalization

Amino acids

Amusements
See also Entertaining; Games; Play; Recreation; Sports;
etc.

Anatomy

Andorra

Anglo-Saxons

Animals
See also Dogs; Horses; etc.

Annapolis

Annuities

Antarctic regions

Anthropology

Antibiotics

Antihistamines.   *See* Histamines

Antiques

Antisemitism.   *See* Jews

Apples

Appraisals.   *See* Valuation

Apportionment

April Fool's Day

Apprentices

Aquariums

Arabia

Arbitration, Industrial

Arbitration, International
    See also Disarmament; International law and relations;
    United Nations

Arbor Day

Archaeology *(American)*

Archery

Architecture
    Details
    Domestic
    History

Archives

Arctic regions

Argentina

Arithmetic
    Study and teaching

Arizona

Arkansas

Armaments
    See also Armies; Disarmament; Munitions of War;
    Navies

Armenia

Armies
    See also United States — Armed forces

Armistice Day

Arms and armor

Army (U. S.) *See* United States — Armed forces; United
States — Army

Art (subdivided by adjective of nationality)
History

Art galleries. *See* Museums

Art treasures in war

Arthritis
See also ACTH (Hormone); Cortisone

Arthur, King

Artificial limbs

Artists

Arts and crafts. *See* Handicraft

Asia. *See* name of individual country, e.g., China; Japan;
etc.

Asphalt

Assessment
See also Taxation; Valuation

Assyria

Astrology

Astronomy

Atheism

Athletics
See also College athletics; Dancing; Games; Physical
education and training; Sports

Atlantic Union. *See* North Atlantic Treaty Organization

Atomic bomb
See also Hiroshima; Hydrogen bomb

Atomic energy
See also Cyclotrons; Uranium

Atypical children

Audio-visual education

Audubon societies. *See* Bird clubs

Aureomycin

Australia

Austria

Authors (subdivided A–Z, by name of author)
See also Poets

Autogiros

Automobile accidents

Automobile drivers
Training

Automobile driving

Automobile industry

Automobile laws and legislation

Automobile parking

Automobile parts

Automobile racing
See also "Hot rods"

Automobile service stations

Automobile trailers. *See* Trailers

Automobile trucks. *See* Motor trucks

Automobiles
See also "Hot rods"; Motor buses; Motor trucks; etc.

Aviation. *See* Aeronautics

Avocados

Azores

B

Babies
See also Infant mortality

Baby-sitting

Babylonia. *See* Iraq

Bach festivals

Backward states

Bacteriology

Bahamas

Bakelite

Balearic Islands

Balkan States. *See* Albania; Bulgaria; Greece; Rumania;
Turkey; Yugoslavia

Ballet

Balloons
See also Airships

Baltic states. *See* Estonia; Finland; Latvia; Lithuania

Bands (Music)

Banking law

Bankruptcy

Banks and banking
See also Building and loan associations; Investments;
Money

Barbados

Barbary states. *See* Algeria; Morocco; Tripoli (Tripolitania); Tunis

Barbecues

Baseball

Basketball

Basketry

Bathrooms

Baths

Batik

Batteries

Bazaars. *See* Fairs

Beauty, Personal

Bedrooms

Bees

Beets and beet sugar

Belgian Congo. *See* Congo, Belgian

Belgium

Bells

Bermuda Islands

Berries

Better Business Bureaus

Bhutan

Bible

Bibliography (*See* under special subjects, also)
    Trade

Bicycling. *See* Cycling

Billboards

Billiards

Bimetalism

Biography (subdivided A–Z, by name of person)
See also Artists; Authors; Chemists; Historians; Historical biography; Musicians; Poets; Scientists; Women, famous; etc.

Biological warfare

Biology

Bird clubs

Bird houses

Birds
See also Poultry
Migration
Songs

Birth control

Birth rate

Black markets

Blind
See also Braille; Dogs as guides; etc.
Schools and institutions

Blood donors

Boards of education

Boats and boating

Bolivia

Bolshevism. *See* Communism

Bomb shelters. *See* Civilian defense

Bonds
Government

Bonus, Soldiers'. *See* Soldiers' bonuses

Book clubs

Book collecting

Book industry and trade

Book reviews

Book selection
  Aids

Book shops. *See* Booksellers and bookselling

Book Week

Bookbinding

Bookmaking. *See* Book industry and trade

Bookmarks

Bookplates

Books, Projected

Books, Talking

Books and reading

Booksellers and bookselling

Borneo (Island)

Bornholm

Bosnia. *See* Yugoslavia

Botany
  Medical

Bottles

Bowling

Boxing

Boy Scouts

Boys

Boys' clubs

Braille

Brazil

Bread

Bricks

Bridge (Game)

Bridges

British Honduras. *See* Honduras, British

Bronzes

Buddhism

✓**Budget**
Business
Household
Municipal
U. S.

Building
Cost

Building and loan associations

Building laws

Building materials

✓**Buildings**
See also Skyscrapers

Bulgaria

Bureaus of educational research
Public schools

Burma

Buses. *See* Motor buses

✓**Business**

Business conditions
See also Economic conditions

Business cycles

Business depression

Business education

Business ethics

Business forecasting

Business letters. *See* Commercial correspondence

Business machines

Business management and organization

Business men

Business recovery

Business research

Business women

Butterflies
    See also Moths

Buttons

Buying habits

C

Cabinet system

Cactus

Calendar

California

Cameos

Camouflage

Camp Fire Girls

Camp meetings

Camps and camping
    See also Summer camps — Educational work

Canada
See also Labrador
Alberta
British Columbia
Manitoba
New Brunswick
Northwest Territories
Nova Scotia
Ontario
Prince Edward Island
Quebec
Saskatchewan
Yukon

Canal Zone

Canals (subdivided by name of canal)

Canary Islands

Canasta (Game)

Cancer

Candy

Canned food

Canning and preserving

Cape Verde Peninsula

Capital punishment

Capitalism

Carbon — Isotopes

Carbon dioxide

Cards
See also Greeting cards

Caricature and cartoons

Carpentry
See also Building

Carving
See also Cameos; Ivory; Soap sculpture; etc.

Castles

Cataloging

Catalogs
Booksellers
Publishers
Trade
Universities and colleges

Catastrophes. *See* Disasters

Cathedrals

Cathode rays

Catholic literature

Catholicism

Cats

Cattle

Cave dwellers and cave dwellings

Caves

Celebes

Cellophane

Cement industry and trade

Cemeteries
Arlington

✓**Censorship**

Census — U. S.
Agriculture
Business
Manufactures
Markets

Miscellaneous
Population
Retail trade
Service establishments
Vital statistics
Wholesale trade

Central America. *See* Costa Rica; Guatemala; Honduras, British; Nicaragua; Panama; Salvador, El

Centralization of control. *See* Consolidation of schools

Ceramics. *See* Pottery

Cereals

Cerebral palsy. *See* Palsy, Cerebral

Certification

Ceylon

Chain letters

Chain stores

Chamber of commerce of the U.S.A.

Chambers of commerce

Character education

Charities

Charters
See also Municipal charters

Checkers

Cheese

Chemical industries
See also Bakelite; Cellophane; "Miracle fabrics"; Varnish and varnishing; etc.

Chemical research

Chemical warfare

Chemicals

Chemistry

Chemistry in war

Chemists

Chess

Chewing gum

Chicago
World's Fair, 1933, 1934

Child Health Day

Child labor

Child placing

Child psychology

Child study

Child welfare

Children
Abnormal
Care and hygiene
Charities, protection, etc. *See* Child welfare
Employment. *See* Child labor
Gifted
Law
Management and training
Nutrition

Children's literature

Children's parties

Children's plays

Children's poetry

Children's songs

Chile

China

Chinchillas

Chinese in the U. S.

Chinese-Japanese wars

Chinese language and literature

Chivalry
See also Feudalism; Knights and knighthood; Middle Ages

Chlorophyll

Chocolate. *See* Cocoa and chocolate

Choric speaking

Chosen. *See* Korea (Chosen)

Christian art and symbolism

Christian science

Christianity

✓ **Christmas**
Customs
Decorations
Music
Poetry
Stories

Church and labor

Church and social problems

Church and state

Church music
Church of Jesus Christ of Latter Day Saints - Pictures
Churches

Cinerama. *See* Moving pictures — Photography

Ciphers and codes

Circus

✓ **Cities and towns**
   Reports

✓ **Citizenship**
   See also Naturalization

Citizenship education

Citrus fruits

City manager plan

City planning
   Zone system

Civics
   See also Citizenship

✓ *Civil Defense*
✓ **Civil rights**

Civil service

Civilian Conservation Camps
   See also Unemployment relief measures — Camps

Civilian defense
   See also Air raids

Civilians in war

Civilization
   See also Art; Costume; etc.

Classical education

Clay modeling

Clay products
   See also Pottery

Cleaning

Cleanliness

Cliff dwellers and dwellings
   See also Man, Prehistoric

Climate

Clocks and watches

Closed shop

Clothing and dress
See also Costume

Club programs
See also special subjects, e.g., American literature;
Music; etc.

Clubs

Coaches and coaching

Coal

Coal miners

Coal mines and mining

Coal-tar products

Coast Guard. *See* United States — Coast Guard

Cocoa and chocolate

Codes (Ciphers). *See* Ciphers and Codes

Coeducation

Coffee

Coins

Cold (Disease)

Collective bargaining. *See* Employees' representation in
government

Collectivism. *See also* Communism; Socialism

Collectors and collecting
See also Book collecting; Coins; Postage stamps; etc.

College athletics

College education
  Cost of

College fraternities

College graduates

College libraries. *See* Libraries, University

College life

College students

Colleges and universities. *See* Universities and colleges

Colombia

Colonial life and customs
  See also Costume; Pilgrim fathers; Puritans; United States — History
Colonization

Colophons

Color

Colorado

Colorado River

Columbus Day

Comics

Commencements

Commerce

Commercial art

Commercial correspondence

Commercial education and business. *See* Business education

Commercial treaties

Commodities

Common market .

Communication
See also various types of communication

Communism
See also Indoctrination; Subversive activities

Community centers

Community chests

Community life

Community surveys

Company unions

Compensation (Law). *See* Workmen's compensation

Compulsory education

Concrete

Conduct of life
See also Character education; Youth

Conducting (Music)

Congo, Belgian

Congress of Industrial Organizations

Connecticut

Conscription

Conservation of resources
See also Forests and forestry; Game protection; National parks and reserves; Soil conservation

Consolidation of schools

Constitution of U. S. *See* United States — Constitution

Constitution Day

Constitutions

Consumer cooperatives

Consumer education

Consumption (Economics)

Contests and contesting

Continuation schools

Contract bridge. *See* Bridge (Game)

Convents and nunneries

Convict labor

Convoy

Cookery

Coolidge, Calvin

Cooperative associations
  See also Consumer cooperatives

Cooperative education

Copper

Copyright

Cork

Corn

Coronations

Corporation law

Corporations
  Reports
  Taxation

Correspondence schools and courses

Corruption (in politics)

Corsica

Cortisone
  See also ACTH (Hormone)

Cosmetics

Cost accounting

Cost of living

Costa Rica

Costume
Design

Cotton
Statistics
Trade

Cottonseed

Counselors and counseling
See also Employees' counselors

Country life

County government

County libraries

Courses of study

Courts
See also Juvenile courts

Crafts. *See* Handicraft

Credit
See also Agricultural credit

Credit unions

Crime and criminals

Crime prevention

Criminal law

Criminal procedure

Criminal psychology

Criminal statistics

Crippled children

Cripples

Crocheting

Cuba (Island)

Cubism

Culture and cultural values

Curricula

Curtains

Cycling

Cyclotrons

Czechoslovakia

D

DDT (Insecticide)

Dairying

Dams

Dancing
See also Ballet; Square-dancing

Daughters of the American Revolution

Deaf
Schools and institutions

Dealer relations

Debating

Debts, Public (subdivided by name of country)

Declaration of Independence

Decoration Day. *See* Memorial Day

Defense. *See* Civilian defense; War defense

Deflation

Degrees, Academic

Delaware

Democracy

Democratic Party

Denmark
See also Bornholm; Funen (Island); Jutland; Zealand

Dentistry
See also Teeth

Department stores

Dependent children. *See* Child placing

Desert

Desertion and non-support

Design

Detectives

Devaluation. *See* Deflation

Devil's Island

Diabetes

Dialogs

Diamonds

Dianetics

Dictaphone

Dictionaries

Diesel engines

Diet

Diplomatic and consular service

Dirigibles. *See* Airships

Disabled — Rehabilitation, etc.

Disarmament

Disasters

Discipline

Discussion, Group

Disease
See also name of disease, e.g. Diabetes

Displaced persons

Dissertations, Academic

Distribution (Economics)

District of Columbia

Divorce

Dogs

Dogs as guides

Dogs in war

Doll festivals

Dolls

Domestic economy. *See* Home economics

Domestic relations courts

Dominican Republic

Drama
See also Theater; etc.

Dramas
See also Dialogs; Monologs; etc.

Dramatists

Dramatization

Draperies

Drawing

Dress.   *See* Clothing and dress; Costume

Drug habit

Drugs
  See also Antibiotics; Histamines; "Miracle drugs"; etc.

Dry goods

Dry ice

Drying (Fruits and vegetables)

Dust

Dust storms

Dutch East Indies.   *See* Netherlands Indies

Dyes and dyeing

Dynamics

E

Ear

Earth

Earthquakes

East

Easter

Eclipses

Economic conditions

Economic planning

Economic policy

Economic research

Economic systems

Economics

Ecuador

Education (subdivided by name of country)
Aims and objectives
Engineering. *See* Engineering education
Experimental. *See* Progressive education
History
Individual
Value. *See also* College education — Value of

Education of women. *See* Woman — Education

Educational law and legislation

Educational periodicals. *See* Periodicals — Educational

Educational psychology

Educational sociology

Educational standards. *See* Standards, educational

Educational surveys

Educators

Efficiency, Industrial

Eggs

Egypt
Sahara

Eisenhower, Dwight D.

Einstein theory

Eire

El Salvador

Elections

Electric apparatus and appliances

Electric furnaces

Electric industries

Electric lighting.   *See* Lighting

Electric machinery

Electric motors

Electric power

Electricity

Electronics

Elementary education

Ellis Island

Emblems, State

Embroidery

Emigration.   *See* Immigration and Emigration

Employees
   Rating

Employees' counselors

Employees' representation in government

Employment

Employment agencies

Employment management

Enamels

Encyclopedias

Endowments

Engineering

Engineering education

Engineers

England
   History

English language

English literature

Entertaining

Entrance examinations and requirements
Universities and colleges

Epilepsy

Epitaphs

Eskimos

Esperanto

Essays

Estonia

Etching

Ethics

Ethiopia

√ **Etiquette**

Eugenics
See also Heredity; Marriage; Sterilization

European recovery program

European War, 1914–1918

European War, 1939–1945
Campaigns and battles
Causes
Hospitals
Maps. *See* Maps
Medical and sanitary affairs
Naval operations
Propaganda
Reparations
Results

Euthanasia

Evangelism

Evergreens

Evolution

Examinations

Exceptional children. *See* Atypical children

Exchange

Executives

Explorers

Explosives

Export trade

Extra-curricular activities

Eye

F

Factory management

Factory schools. *See* Vocational education

Fairs
  See also Festivals

Fairy tales

Faith

Family

Family allowances. *See* Budget — Household

Family life
  Education for

Famines

Fans

Farm life.   *See* Country life

Farm market

Farm subsidies

Farm tenancy

Father's Day

Fathers

Fatigue

Fats.   *See* Oils and fats

Federal aid for education

Federal reserve system

Feeble-minded

Felt

Ferns

Fertilizers

Festivals
   See also name and type of festival, e.g. Bach festivals;
   Doll festivals

Fetishism

Feudalism

Fiction

Fiji Islands

Files and filing (Documents, etc.)

Films, Educational.   *See* Audio-visual education

Finance
   City schools
   International
   United States
   Universities and colleges

Finger prints

Finland

Fire marks

Fire prevention

Fire protection

Firemen
Training

Fireplaces
See also Barbecues
Accessories
Mantels
Modern

Fires

First aid in illness and injury

Fish (as food)

Fisheries

Fishes
Aquariums
Tropical

Fishing

Flag Day

Flags

Flax

Floats

Flood prevention and control

Floods

Floor coverings
See also Rugs

Floors

Floriculture

Florida

Flowers
  See also Wildflowers
  Arrangement of
  Artificial

Flying Saucers

Folger Shakespeare Library

Folk songs

Folklore

Food
  Canned
  Frozen

Food laws and legislation

Football

Forecasting, Business. *See* Business forecasting

Foreign exchange. *See* Exchange

Foreign service. *See* Diplomatic and consular service

Foreign-speaking children

Foreign students in the U. S.

Foreign trade. *See* Commerce

Foremen training

Forest products

Forests and forestry
  See also Trees

Formosa

Forts

Fortune telling

Fossils

Foster homes. *See* Child placing

Foundations, Charitable and educational

Foundries

Four freedoms

Fourth of July

France
See also Madagascar

Fraternities. *See* College fraternities; High school fraternities

Free enterprise

Free speech. *See* Speech, Freedom of

Free will and determinism

Freedom
See also Academic freedom; Four freedoms; Free will and determinism; Liberty; Press, Freedom of; Speech, Freedom of

Freedom Train

Freezers and freezing
See also Food — Frozen

Freight and freightage

French literature

French Pacific Settlements

Freshmen

Friends, Society of. *See* Quakers

Frogs

Fruit
See also Apples; Berries; Citrus fruits; etc.

Fuel
See also Coal, Petroleum

Funen (Island)

Funeral services

Fur

Furniture
See also Upholstery

G

Gambling

Game protection

Games

Garages

Garden clubs

Gardening

Gardens

Gas
　Natural

Gasoline
　Taxation

Gasoline industry

Gasoline service stations.　*See* Automobile service stations

Geiger-Müller counters

Gems.　*See* Precious stones; Zircons

Genealogy

Genius

Geography

Geology

Geopolitics

Georgia

German literature

Germans in the U. S.

Germany
National Socialist Movement
Western

Gesso

Ghosts

Gibralter

Gift-wrapping

Gilds

Gipsies

Girl Scouts

Girls

Girls' clubs

Glands
See also Hormones

Glass industry

Glass painting and staining

Glassware

Gliders

Glossaries

Glue

Gold (as money)

Gold mines and mining

Golf

Golf courses

Gourds

Government appropriations and expenditures
See also Budget — U. S.

Government competition with business

Government employees

Government investigations
See also Amerasia case; Crime and criminals; Hiss case; Loyalty investigations

Government ownership

Government publications

Grade crossings

Graduate schools

Grain trade

Grapes

Graphology

Grasses

Great Books Program

Great Britain.   *See* England; Ireland; Scotland; Wales; etc.

Great Lakes

Greece

Greece, Ancient

Greek letter societies.   *See* College fraternities; High school fraternities

Greek literature

Greenhouses

Greenland

Greeting cards

Grocery trade

Grottoes.   *See* Caves

Group discussion.   *See* Discussion, Group

Guadalcanal

Guam

Guatemala

Guianas (includes British, French Guianas)

Guided missiles.   *See* Missiles, Guided

Guilds.   *See* Gilds

Guineas (includes Portuguese, Spanish Guineas)

Guns

Gymnasiums

Gypsies.   *See* Gipsies

Gyroscope

H

Haiti

Hallowe'en

Handicapped

Handicraft

Hardware

Hats

Hawaiian Islands

Hay fever

Health

Health clinics

Health demonstrations

Health education

Health insurance. *See* Insurance, Health

Health service

Hearing
   See also Deaf; Ear

Heart

Heating
   See also Fireplaces

Helicopters

Heliotherapy

Helium

Heraldry
   See also Bookplates

Herbs

Heredity

Hides and skins

High school fraternities

High schools

Higher education
   See also Scholarships and fellowships; Universities and colleges; etc.

Highway transportation

Hiroshima

Hiss case

Histamines

Historians

Historical biography

Historical drama

Historical fiction

Historical research

History
See also United States — History; etc.
Ancient
Modern

Hitler, Adolf. *See* Germany — National Socialist Movement

Hobbies
See also name of hobby

Hogs

Holding companies

Holidays
See also name of holiday

Holland. *See* Netherlands

Home

Home economics
See also School lunches

Home ownership

Homesteads
See also Subsistence homesteads

Honduras

Honduras, British

Honey

Honor systems. *See* Student self-government

Honors course

Hoover, Herbert

Hoover War Library

Hormones
  See also ACTH (Hormone) ; Cortisone

Hornbooks

Horsemanship

Horses
  Racing
  Shows

Hospitals
  Military
  See also United States — Veterans administration —
    Hospitals

"Hot rods"

Hotels

Hours of labor

House decoration. *See* Interior decoration

House organs

House plants

Household appliances
  See also Electric apparatus and appliances

Houses, Prefabricated

Housing
  Cooperative

Housing laws and legislation

Human relations

Humane societies

Humanism

Humor
American

Hungary

Hurricanes

Hydro-electric power

Hydrogen bomb

Hygiene
See also Health education

Hymns

Hypnotism

I

Ice

Ice-skating

Iceberg patrol. *See* International Ice Patrol

Icebergs

Iceland

Idaho

Illegitimacy

Illinois

Illiteracy

Illumination of books and manuscripts

Illustrators

Immigrants in the U. S.
See also Displaced persons; Refugees

Immigration and emigration

Immortality

Imperialism

Inaugurations
Balls

Income

Income tax

Incunabula

Index numbers

India
See also Pakistan

India rubber. *See* Rubber

Indiana

Indians

Indians of North America

Individualism

Indo-Chinese Federation
See also Burma; Siam; etc.

Indoctrination

Indonesia
See also Celebes; Sumatra

Indoor plants. *See* House plants

Industrial chemistry. *See* Chemical industries

Industrial education
See also Vocational education

Industrial efficiency. *See* Efficiency, Industrial

Industrial hygiene. *See* Occupational diseases

Industrial management

Industrial progress

Industrial relations

Industrial research

Industry
  See also name of industry

Industry and education

Infant mortality

Infantile paralysis

Inflation (Finance)

Insane
  Care and treatment

Insecticides
  See also DDT (Insecticide)

Insects

Installment plan

Insurance
  See also Workmen's compensation

Insurance, Accident

Insurance, Group

Insurance, Health

Insurance, Life

Insurance, Social
  See also Insurance, Unemployment; Old age pensions

Insurance, Unemployment

Intelligence tests
  See also Tests and scales

Interior decoration
  See also Furniture

International education

International Ice Patrol

International law and relations

Interplanetary voyages

Interview (Employment)

Inventions

Inventors

Investment banking

Investment trusts

Investments
  Foreign

Iowa

Iran

Iraq

Ireland
  See also Eire; Northern Ireland

Irish literature

Iron industry and trade

Irrigation

Islands
  See also name of island

Isle of Man

Israel

Italian literature

Italian Somaliland

Italians in the U. S.

Italy

Ivory

J

Jade

Jamaica

Japan
    See also Formosa; etc.
    Reconstruction

Japanese in the U. S.

Java

Jesus Christ

Jet propulsion
    See also Airplanes, Jet propelled; Missiles, Guided

Jewelry
    See also Precious stones; Zircons; etc.

Jews
    Religion. *See* Judaism

Jews in Germany

Jews in the U. S.

Jiu-jitsu

Jokes

Jordan

Journalism

Judaism

Jugoslavia. *See* Yugoslavia

Junior colleges

Junior high schools

Jutland

Juvenile courts

Juvenile delinquency

K

Kansas

Kentucky

Kenya

Kindergarten-primary education

Kitchens

Kites

Knights and knighthood
See also Chivalry

Knitting

Kongo, Belgian.   *See* Congo, Belgian

Korea (Chosen)

Korea — Civil War, 1950–

Ku Klux Klan

L

Labels

Labor and capital

Labor and laboring classes
See also Child labor ; Migrant labor ; Strikes ; Wages ; etc

Labor Day

Labor laws and legislation
See also name of law, e.g. Taft-Hartley Act, 1947

Labor party (Great Britain)

Labor turnover

Labor unions. *See* Trade unions

Labrador

Lace

Lake dwellers and lake dwellings

Lakes
    See also Great Lakes; under name of country; etc.

Lamps

Land

Land banks

Land-grant colleges

Landscape gardening

Language, Universal
    See also Esperanto

Language and languages

Lapland

Latin America

Latin language and literature

Latvia

Laundry

Law

Lead

League of Nations

Learning and scholarship

Leases

Leather

Leather work

Leaves of absence

Lebanon

Legal aid

Legislative assemblies

Leisure

Letter writing
See also Commercial correspondence

Lettering

Liberalism

Liberia

Liberty

Liberty, Statue of

Librarians

Libraries
See also County libraries; School libraries; etc.
Reports
Supplies

Libraries, Special

Libraries, University

Library administration

Library architecture

Library laws

Library of Congress

Library schools and training

Library science

Libya

Lie detectors

Liechtenstein

Life insurance. *See* Insurance, Life

Light

Lighthouses

Lighting
  See also Lamps

Lime

Lincoln, Abraham

Linen
  Household

Linoleum

Liquor laws and legislation

Liquor problem
  See also Prohibition

Literary prizes. *See* Rewards, prizes, etc.

Lithuania

Livestock
  See also Cattle; Hogs; Horses; Sheep; etc.

Loan funds. *See* Student loans and loan funds

Loans

Lobbying

Local government
  See also County government

Locomotives

Logic

Logistics

London

Longevity
See also Old age

Lotteries

Louisiana

Love

Loyalty, Oaths of

Loyalty investigations

Lumber
See also Forests and forestry

Luxemburg

Luzon (Island)

Lynching

M

MacArthur, Douglas

McGuffey readers

Machinery
See also Agricultural machinery; Machinery in industry; Tools; Weapons

Machinery in industry

Madagascar

Madeira

Magic

Maine

Malta

Man

Man, Isle of. *See* Isle of Man

Man, Prehistoric
  See also Cliff dwellers and dwellings; Lake dwellers and lake dwellings; etc.

Management
  See also Business management and organization; Factory management; Industrial management

Manchuria

Manganese

Manufactures

Manuscripts

Maple sugar

Maps (subdivided by name of country; etc.)

Marble

Marine Corps. *See* United States — Marine Corps

Marine engines

Marionettes. *See* Puppets and puppet plays

Market surveys

Marketing
  Cooperative

Marketing, Cooperative
  See also Cooperative associations

Markets, Roadside

Marriage

Maryland

Masks (facial)

Massachusetts

Matches

Maternity welfare

Mathematicians

Mathematics

May Day

Measurement
See also Metric system

Meat

Meat industry and trade

Mechanical drawing

Medical education

Medical plants. *See* Botany — Medical; Herbs

Medical research

Medical service, Cost of

Medicine

Medicine, Psychosomatic

Memorial Day

Memory

Men, Famous
See also name of group, e.g. Scientists

Mental hygiene
See also Dianetics

Menus and recipes

Merchandising

Merchant Marine

Mesopotamia. *See* Iraq

Metal work

Metals
  See also name of metal

Meteorology. *See* Weather

Meteors

Metric system

Metropolitan Opera Company

Mexicans in the U. S.

Mexico

Michigan

Microphotography

Microscopy

Middle-aged workers

Middle Ages

Midway Islands

Migrant labor

Military education

Military service, Compulsory

Military training camps

Milk

Milk, Evaporated

Mimeographing

Mineralogy
  See also Precious stones; Zircons; etc.

Mines and mineral resources
  See also Coal mines and mining; Gold mines and mining;
  etc.

Minnesota

Minorities

"Miracle drugs"
See also ACTH (Hormone); Antibiotics; Aureomycin;
Cortisone; Histamines; Sulfa (Drug); etc.

"Miracle fabrics"
See also Nylon; Orlon

Miracle, morality and mystery plays

Mirrors

Missiles, Guided

Missionaries

Missions

Mississippi

Missouri

Molasses

Monaco

Monasteries

Money
See also Coins

Mongolia

Monologs

Monopolies

Monroe Doctrine

Montana

Montenegro. *See* Yugoslavia

Moon. *See* Astronomy

Mormonism

Morocco

Mortality

Mosaics

Mother Goose. *See* Nursery rhymes

Mother's Day

Mothers' pensions

Moths
  See also Butterflies

Motor buses

Motor trucks

Motor vehicles
  Laws and regulations

Mound builders and mounds

Mount Palomar Observatory

Mount Rushmore National Memorial

Mount Wilson Observatory

Mouth hygiene

Moving picture actors and actresses

Moving picture plays

Moving pictures
  Photography
  Stereoscopic

Municipal accounting

Municipal charters

Municipal finance
  See also Budget — Municipal

Municipal government

Municipal ownership

Municipal reports
See also Cities and towns — Reports

Municipal universities and colleges

Munitions of war

Muscle Shoals project. *See* Tennessee Valley Project

Museums

Mushrooms

Music
See also Bach festivals; Church music; Opera; Orchestra; Phonograph records; Songs; etc.

Music, Influence of

Music week

Musical instruments

Musicians

Mythology

N

NATO. *See* North Atlantic Treaty Organization

Names, Geographical

Names, Personal

Narcotics
See also Drug habit

National characteristics

National conventions (Political)

National Labor Relations Act, 1937

National Labor Relations Board

National monuments
See also name of monument

National parks and reserves

Nationalism and nationality

Naturalization

Nature

Nature study

Naval bases

Navies

Navy — U. S. *See* United States — Navy

Nazi party. *See* Germany — National Socialist Movement

Near East

Nebraska

Needlework
  See also Knitting; Sewing; Tatting; etc.

Negro literature

Negro songs

Negroes

Negroes in the U. S.
  Education
  Employment
  Hospitals

Nepal

Netherlands

Netherlands Indies

Neuroses

Nevada

New Caledonia

"New Deal"

New Guinea (includes British New Guinea and Dutch New Guinea)

New Hampshire

New Hebrides

New Jersey

New Mexico

New York (State)

New York (City)
　Description

New York Stock Exchange.　*See* Stock Exchange (New York City)

New Zealand
　North Island
　South Island

Newfoundland
　See also Labrador

Newsboys

Newspaper work.　*See* Journalism

Newspapers

Nicaragua

Nickel

Nigeria

Nitrates

Nitrogen

Noise

Noise abatement

Normal schools and teachers colleges

North

North Atlantic Treaty Organization

North Carolina

North Dakota

North Island. *See* New Zealand

Northern Ireland

Northwest

Norway

Nova Scotia

Novels. *See* Fiction

Nursery rhymes

Nursery schools

Nurses and nursing

Nutrition

Nylon

O

Oak Ridge, Tennessee

Occupational diseases

Occupational therapy

Occupations
See also Vocational guidance
Diseases and hygiene. *See* Occupational diseases

Ocean

Ocean travel

Oceania

Office management

Office workers

Ohio

Oil burners

Oil tidelands.   *See* Tidelands, Oil

Oil wells.   *See* Petroleum

Oils and fats

Oklahoma

Old age

Old age pensions

Older workers

Oleomargarine

Olives

Olympic games

Open and closed shop

Open-air schools

Opera
   See also Metropolitan Opera Company

Opportunity schools

Optometry

Orations

Orchestra

Ordnance

Oregon

Organ

Orlon

Orphans and orphan asylums

Osteopathy

Outer Mongolia (Mongolian People's Republic)

Oysters

P

Pacific Islands.   *See* Oceania

Packaging

Packing industry

Pageants

Painters.   *See* Artists

Painting

Pakistan

Palaces

Palestine

Palsy, Cerebral

Pan America.   *See* Latin America

Panama

Panama Canal

Panics
   See also Business depression

Paper

Paper making and trade

Paper work

Parachutes

Parades

Paraguay

Paralysis, Cerebral. *See* Palsy, Cerebral

Parent-child relationships

Parent education

Parent-teacher associations

Paris

Parks
  See also National parks and reserves

Parliamentary practice

Parliaments

Parochial schools

Parole. *See* Probation system

Part-time education

Parties. *See* Entertaining; Games

Passion plays

Patents

Patriotism

Peace

Peanuts

Pearl Harbor, Attack on, 1941

Pearls

Penmanship

Pennsylvania

Pens

Pensions
  See also Mothers' pensions; Old-age pensions; Soldiers'
  bonuses
  Industrial

Periodicals
Educational

Permanent Court of International Justice
History

Persia. *See* Iran

Personality

Peru

Petroleum

Petroleum products

Pets
See also Cats; Dogs; etc.

Pewter

Phi Beta Kappa

Philanthropy

Philippines, Republic of

Philosophy

Phonetics

Phonograph records

Phosphates

Photoengraving

Photography
See also Microphotography; Photostat; Telephotography;
etc.

Photostat

Physical education and training

Physics

Physiology
See also Anatomy; Old age; etc.

Piano

Picture books

Pictures
Arrangement of

Pigeons

Pilgrim fathers

Pilgrims and pilgrimages
See also Saints

Pineapples

Pipe organ.   *See* Organ

Planetariums

Plants
See also Flowers; Herbs; Weeds; etc.
Soilless culture

Plastics

Platforms, Political

Plating

Platinum

Play

Playgrounds

Playing cards.   *See* Cards

Plays.   *See* Dramas

Plumbing

Poetry

Poets

Point four program.   *See* United States — Technical
assistance program

Poland

Police

Poliomyelitis. *See* Infantile paralysis

Political campaigns

Political conventions. *See* National conventions (Political)

Political corruption. *See* Corruption (in politics)

Political parties
  See also name of party; Platforms, Political; Political campaigns

Political science

Politics

Pony express

Poor laws

Popes

Population. *See* Census — U. S. — Population

Population problems

Porcelain. *See* Pottery

Portugal

Postage stamps

Postal rates

Postal service
  History

Posture

Potash

Pottery

Poultry

Power
See also Atomic energy; Electric power; Water power; etc.

Practice teaching

Prayer

Preceptorial system. *See* Honors course

Precious stones
See also Diamonds; Jade; Pearls; etc.

Pregnancy

Prejudice

Presidential candidates

Presidents — U. S.
See also name of president

Press, Freedom of

Prices
Control

Primaries

Principals
Elementary schools
High schools

Printing

Printing industry

Prints

Prison labor. *See* Convict labor

Prisoners

Prisoners of war

Prisons

Probation system

Production

Profession, Choice of
See also Occupations; Vocational guidance

Profit sharing

Progress

Progressive education

Prohibition

Project method in teaching

Promotion
Students

Propaganda
See also Indoctrination

Prophecies

Prostitution

Proteins

Protestantism

Protons

Proving grounds
See also name of Proving ground, e.g. White Sands proving grounds

Pseudonyms and antonyms

Psychiatry

Psychical research

Psychoanalysis

Psychological clinics

Psychologists

Psychology

Psychosomatic medicine. *See* Medicine, Psychosomatic

Public administration

Public debts. *See* Debts, Public

Public health

Public opinion
  Polls

Public relations

Public service

Public speaking. *See also* Speech

Public utilities

Public welfare

Public works

Publishers and publishing

Puerto Rico

Puppets and puppet plays

Purchasing

Puritans
  See also Pilgrim fathers

Pyramids

Q

Quacks and quackery

Quakers

Quilts

Quotations

R

Race problems
  See also Minorities; Negroes; etc.

Races of man

Racketeering

Radar

Radio

Radio advertising

Radio broadcasting

Radio in education

Radio in war

Radio industry

Radio stations

Radio telegraphy

Radioactivity
See also Geiger-Müller counters

Radiocarbon. *See* Carbon — Isotopes

Radium

Railroads

Railroads and state — U. S.

Rain

Rats

Rayon. *See* Silk, Artificial

Reading

Readings

Real estate

Real property

Recesses, School

Reclamation of land

Reconstruction

Recreation
See also Community centers; Games; Sports; etc.

Red Cross

Reference books

Reform

Reformatories

Refrigeration and refrigerating machinery

Refugees
See also Displaced persons

Regional planning

Registration
Universities and colleges

Rehabilitation. *See* Disabled, Rehabilitation, etc.

Religion

Religion and science

Religious education

Repairing

Report cards

Reproduction

Reptiles. *See also* Snakes

Republican party

Research
See also name of type of research, e.g. Medical research

Retail trade

Revolutions

Rewards, prizes, etc.

Rhode Island

Rice

Rivers
See also under name of country

Roads
See also Highway transportation

Roadside improvement

Rockets
See also Jet propulsion; Missiles, Guided

Romanticism

Rome, Ancient

Roosevelt, Franklin D.

Roosevelt, Theodore

Rope

Rubber

Rubber industry and trade
See also Tires

Rugs

Rumania

Rural schools

Rural surveys

Russia.   *See* Union of Soviet Socialist Republics

S

Sabotage

Safety education

Safety organization

Sahara.   *See* Egypt — Sahara

Saint Patrick's Day

Saint Valentine's Day.   *See* Valentine Day

Saints

Sales management

Sales tax

Salesmen and salesmanship

Salmon

Salt

Salvador, El

Salvage (Waste)

Salvation Army

Samoa, American.   *See* American Samoa

San Marino

Sanitation
    School buildings

Sardinia

Satellite states

Saudi Arabia, Kingdom of

Saving and thrift

Scales

Scandinavia.   *See* Denmark; Norway; Sweden

Scandinavian literature

Scenarios.   *See* Moving picture plays

Scholarship.   *See* Learning and scholarship

Scholarships and fellowships

School banks

School children
Food. *See* School lunches

School discipline. *See* Discipline

School finance. *See* Finance — City schools

School grounds

School libraries

School lunches

School nurses

School orchestra

School surveys. *See* Educational surveys

Schoolhouses
Equipment

Schools
See also name of type of school, e.g. Technical schools
Rating

Science
See also name of science, e.g. Astronomy

Scientific research

Scientists

Scotland

Scottish literature

Scouts and scouting. *See* Boy Scouts; Girl Scouts

Screens

Scrip. *See* Money

Sculptors

Sculpture

Sea. *See* Ocean

Sea songs

Sea stories

Seabees. *See* United States — Seabees

Seals
  City
  College
  State

Secondary education

Secretaries

Securities

Seeds

"Seeing Eye" dogs. *See* Dogs as guides

Seven wonders of the world

Sewage

Sewing

Sex hygiene
  See also Reproduction

Sex instruction

Shakespeare, William

Sheep

Shipbuilding

Shipping

Ships
  Historic
  Models

Shipwrecks

Shoe industry and trade

Shoes

Shopping centers

Short selling. *See* Speculation

Short story

Show windows

Shrines

Shrubs

Siam

Siberia

Sicily

Signals and signaling

Signs

Silk

Silk, Artificial

Silk industry

Silver

Silverware

Skating
   See also Ice-skating

Skyscrapers

Slavery

Sleep

Slip-covers

Smallpox

Smog

Smoke

Smoke prevention

Smoking (Habit)

Snakes

Snow

Soap

Soap sculpture

Soccer

Social agencies

Social hygiene

Social justice

Social laws and legislation

Social progress

Social sciences

Social security

Social service. *See* Social work

Social statistics

Social surveys

Social work

Socialism
    See also Collectivism; Communism

Sociology

Sociology, Rural

Soil conservation

Soils

Soldiers
    See also Veterans

Soldiers' bonuses

Songs
  See also Sea songs; etc.

Soul

Sound
  See also Ear; Hearing

South

South America. *See* Argentina; Bolivia; Brazil; Chile; Colombia; Ecuador; Panama; Paraguay; Peru; Uruguay; Venezuela

South Carolina

South Dakota

South Island. *See* New Zealand — South Island

Southwest

Spain

Spanish literature

Speaking. *See* Debating; Orations; Speech; etc.

Speculation

Speech

Speech, Freedom of

Speech defects

Speech education

Spelling

Spices

Spiders

Spies

Spinning

Spiritualism

Spitzbergen

Sponges

Spoons. *See* Silverware

Sports
  See also Games ; name of sport

Spraying and dusting

Square-dancing

Stabilization in industry

Stage lighting

Stage scenery

Stained glass. *See* Glass painting and staining

Stamps. *See* Postage stamps

Standard of living

Standardization

Standards, Educational

Stars. *See* Astrology ; Astronomy

State appropriations for education

State governments

Statistics. *See* name of type of statistics, e.g. Social
  Statistics

Steel
  Stainless

Steel industry and trade

Stereophotography
  See also Moving Pictures — Stereoscopic

Sterilization

Stock exchange (New York City)

Stone

Storms
See also Hurricanes; Rain; Snow; etc.

Story-telling

Straits Settlements

Street cleaning

Street railroads
Fares

Strikes

Student activities. *See* Extra-curricular activities

Student advisers and counselors. *See* Counselors and
counseling

Student loans and loan funds

Student self-government

Student teaching. *See* Practice teaching

Students
High schools
Universities and colleges

Study

Stunts

Submarines

Subsistence homesteads

Subversive activities
See also United States — Congress — House of Representatives — Special Comm. on un-American activities

Sugar
See also Beets and beet sugar; Maple sugar

Suicide

Sulfa (Drug)

Sumatra

Summer camps
Educational work

Summer schools

Sun

Sundials

Superstition

Supervision of teaching

Supreme Court of U. S.

Surplus, War

Surveying

Surveys. *See* Educational surveys ; Public opinion — Polls ;
Social surveys

Sweden

Swimming

Swimming pools

Switzerland

Swords

Symbolism. *See* Christian art and symbolism

Symphonies

Syria

T

Table

Table ware. *See* Silverware

Taft-Hartley Act, 1947

Talc

Tapestries

Tariff

Tasmania

Tatting

Taxation
  See also Income tax; Sales tax; etc.

Taxation for education

Taxidermy

Tea

Teacher placement

Teacher training

Teachers

Teachers' associations

Teachers
  Agencies
  High schools
  Reading
  Salaries, pensions, etc.
  Training
  Universities and colleges

Teachers colleges. *See* Normal schools and teachers colleges

Teaching

Teaching aids

Teaching loads

Technical education

Technical schools

Technocracy

Technological unemployment

Teeth

Telegraph

Telephone

Telephotography

Telescope

Television
　Aids and devices
　Color
　Educational applications

Television broadcasting

Temperance
　See also Alcoholism; Prohibition

Tennessee

Tennessee Valley Project

Tennis

Terrariums

Territorial waters

Territory of the Pacific Islands

Tests and scales

Texas

Textbooks

Textiles
　See also name of fabric; "Miracle fabrics"

Textile industry

Thanksgiving Day

Theater

Theater, Little

Theology
  See also Religion; etc.

Therapeutics

Thermometers

Thousand Islands

Thread

Three dimensional moving pictures. *See* Moving pictures — Stereoscopic

Thrift. *See* Saving and thrift

Tibet

Tidelands, Oil

Tiles

Time
  See also Clocks and watches

Tin

Tires

Tobacco
  See also Smoking (Habit)

Tools
  See also Agricultural machinery; Weapons; etc.
  Prehistoric

Tornadoes

Totems

Toys
  See also Dolls

Trade-marks

Trade unions
See also Company unions

Traffic regulations
See also Motor vehicles — Laws and regulations

Trailers

Trans-Jordan

Transportation
See also name of type of transportation, e.g. Automobiles

Trapping

Travel

Traveler's Aid

Treaties. *See* United States — Foreign relations

Tree dwellers and tree dwellings

Trees
Blossoms
Historic
Leaves

Trieste, Free Territory of

Tripoli (Tripolitania)

Truman, Harry S.

Trusts

Trusts, Industrial

Truth

Tuberculosis

Tumors

Tunis

Tunnels

Turkey

Tutorial system. *See* Honors course

Typewriters

Typewriting

U

UNESCO

Un-American activities. *See* Subversive activities;
United States — Congress — House of Representatives
— Special Comm. on un-American activities

Unemployment

Unemployment insurance. *See* Insurance, Unemployment

Unemployment relief measures
Camps

Uniforms and insignia

Union of South Africa

Union of Soviet Socialist Republics

Unions. *See* Trade unions

United Nations
See also UNESCO

United States
See also name of state
Aeronautics
Air Force
Army
Navy
Antiquities
Armed forces
See also name of special service, e.g. United States —
Air Force
Army
Cabinet
Civilization

Coast Guard
Commerce
Congress
    House of Representatives
        Special Comm. on un-American activities
    Senate
Constitution
    Amendments
    Amendments, Proposed
Defenses
Description and travel
Economic conditions
Economic history
Economic policy
Finance
Foreign population
Foreign relations
History
Industries and government
Marine Corps
Navy
Politics and government
Population
    Statistics.   *See* Census — U. S. — Population
    Presidents.   *See* Presidents — U. S.
Seabees
Social conditions
Technical assistance program
Veterans administration
    Hospitals
Women's Army Corps

Units of Work

Universal military training.   *See* Military service, Compulsory

Universities and colleges

University extension
    See also Adult education; Correspondence schools and courses

Upholstery

Uranium

Uruguay

Utah

Utopias

V

Vacation schools

Valentine Day

Valuation

Vanadium

Varnish and varnishing

Vatican

Vegetables

Venereal diseases

Venezuela

Vermont

Veterans
   See also American Legion

Veterinary medicine

Victorian period

Vice

Vines

Violin

Virgin Islands

Virginia

Viruses

Visual education. *See* Audio-visual education

Vital statistics

Vitamins

Vivisection

Vocational education
   See also Opportunity schools

Vocational guidance

Voice

"Voice of America" (Radio program)

Volcanoes

Voting

W

Wages

Wagner Act. *See* National Labor Relations Act, 1937

Wales

Wall coverings

Wall decoration

War
   See also name of war

War, Cost of. *See* Debts, Public

War, Outlawry of

War defense

War surplus. *See* Surplus, War

Warehouses

Warfare
   See also Biological warfare; Chemical warfare

Washington, George

Washington (State)

Washington (D. C.)

Water pollution

Water power

Water-supply

Waterways

Waterworks

Wealth

Weapons
See also Guns

Weather
See also Hurricanes; Rain; Snow; Storms; etc.

Weather lore

Weather vanes

Weaving

Weddings

Weeds

Weights and measures
See also Scales

Welding

Welfare state

West

West Indies

West Point Military Academy

West Virginia

Westminster Abbey

Whaling

Wheat

White Sands proving grounds

Wholesale trade

Wight, Isle of

Wildflowers

Williamsburg, Virginia

Wills

Wilson's fourteen points

Wind tunnels

Wine

Wire

Wisconsin

Woman
 Crime
 Education
 Employment
 Health and hygiene
 Occupations
 Social and moral questions

Women, Famous

Women and politics

Women as athletes

Women as aviators

Women as journalists

Women as physicians

Women in war service
  See also United States — Women's Army Corps

Wood

Wood engravings

Woodworking

Wool

Woolen and worsted manufacture

Words

Workmen's compensation

World Court. *See* Permanent Court of International
  Justice

World Federation

World War. *See* European War, 1914–1918; European
  War, 1939–1945

Wrestling

Writing

Wyoming

X

X–Ray

Y

Yachts and yachting

Yarn

Young Men's Christian Association

Young Women's Christian Association

Youth

Youth in war

Yugoslavia

Z

Zealand

Zeppelins. *See* Airships

Zinc

Zircons

Zoning. *See* City planning — Zone system

Zoos

SUBDIVISIONS FOR LOCAL MATERIAL: CITY, COUNTY AND STATE

(* State, in addition to the other local subdivisions possible)

A

*Accidents
See also Safety education; Traffic regulations

Accounting department

*Adult education

*Advertising
See also Publicity

*Aeronautics

*Agriculture

*Airports

*Animals

Annexations

Annual reports. *See* Reports

Antique shops

*Antiquities

Appraisals

*Arbor Day

*Archaeology

*Architecture

Armory

*Art

Art associations

Art institute

*Artists

*Audio-visual education

*Authors

B

*Banks and banking

*Bar association

*Beaches

*Beautification
See also Parks and reserves; Playgrounds; etc.

Better Business Bureau

*Biography (subdivided A–Z)
See also Artists; Authors; Musicians; etc.

*Birds

*Blind

Board of education

*Botanical gardens

*Boundaries

Boy Scouts

Boys' clubs

*Bridges

Broadcasting.   *See* Radio broadcasting; Television broadcasting

Budget.   *See* Finance

*Building
See also Housing; Real estate

*Building code

Building department

Buildings.   *See* Architecture

*Business conditions

C

*Camps

*Canals

Cemeteries

Censorship

*Census
   See also Population; Vital statistics; etc.

*Centennial

Chamber of commerce

*Charities
   See also Community chest; name of charity, e.g. Salvation Army

*Charter (including amendments)
   See also Ordinances

*Child labor

*Child placing

*Child welfare

Christmas

*Churches
   See also Missions

*Cities and towns (subdivided A–Z)

Citizenship
   See also Naturalization

City attorney

City clerk

City council

City employees

City manager

City officials

City planning

*****Civil service**

*****Civilian defense**

*****Climate**

*****Clubs**
See also name of club

Colleges and universities.   *See* Universities and colleges

*****Communication**

Community chest

Congressional districts.   *See* Legislative districts

*****Congressmen**

*****Conservation of resources**
See also Forests and forestry; Game protection; Soil
conservation

*****Constitution**

*****Cooperatives**

*****Corporations**
See also name of corporation

Council.   *See* City council

Counties (subdivided A–Z)

County offices

*****Court houses**

*Courts

Credit bureau

Credit union

*Crime and criminals

*Cripples

*Customs

D

*Dams

*Deaf

*Defectives

Defense.   *See* Civilian defense

Department stores

Description
      See also Maps

Directories

Disabled — Rehabilitation, etc.
      See also Blind; Cripples; Deaf; Defectives; Handi-
      capped; etc.

Disaster council

*Divorce

*Documents

*Drama
      See also Festivals; Fiestas; Theaters; etc.

E

*Economic conditions

*Education
      See also Adult education; Audio-visual education; Board

of education; Teachers; Universities and colleges; Vocational education; etc.

*Elections (subdivided by year)
See also City officials; Congressmen; etc.

*Employees
See also City employees

*Employment

Engineering department

F

*Fairs
See also Festivals; Fiestas; name of fair

Farms. *See* Agriculture

*Festivals

*Fiestas

*Finance
See also Taxation

*Fire department

*Fires and fire prevention

*Fisheries

*Fishing

*Flag, State

Floats

*Flood prevention and control
See also Dams

*Floods

*Flower, State

Flower shows

*Flowers

*Flowers, Wild

*Folklore

*Food adulteration and inspection

Foreign trade

*Forests and forestry

*Freeways

*Fruit industry

*Fuel supply

G

Galleries and museums. *See* Art institute; Museums

*Gambling and vice

*Game protection

Garbage disposal

Gardens and gardening

Geography
  See also Description; Maps

Girl Scouts

Girls' clubs

Golf courses

Goodwill Industries

*Governor

*Governor's mansion

H

*Handicapped
  See also Blind; Cripples; Deaf; Defectives; Disabled —
  Rehabilitation, etc.

*Harbors

*Health

*Health department

Highways. *See* Freeways; Roads

*Historic houses

*Historic landmarks

*Historical societies

*History

*Hospitals
  See also State hospitals

Hotels

*Housing

Humane society

*Hunting
  See also Game protection

Hygiene

I

*Illegitimacy

*Income tax

*Industries
  See also Products

*Institutions
  See also State hospitals

Insurance

*Insurance, Unemployment

Inventions

Inventors

*Islands

J

Jails

Jews

Junior colleges

*Justice, Administration of
See also Courts

*Juvenile delinquency

L

*Labor
See also Child labor; Migratory workers; Wages; etc.

*Labor unions. *See* Trade unions

*Lakes

*Lands
See also Tidelands

Law library. *See* Libraries

*Laws

Lawyers

*Legislative districts

*Legislature

*Library associations

*Libraries

*Licenses

*Liquor problem

Little theaters. *See* Theaters

M

Manufactures. *See* Industries; Products

*Maps

*Market research

*Markets

*Marriage

Merchants' association

*Migratory workers

*Milk control

*Military training

*Mines and mineral resources

*Missions

*Money

*Moral conditions
   See also Gambling and vice

*Motor vehicles — Laws and regulations

*Mountains

Municipal activities

*Museums

*Music

*Musicians

N

*Names

*National parks.   *See* Parks and reserves

*Naturalization

*Negroes

*Newspapers

Nursery schools

O

Officials. *See* City officials; etc.

Oil wells. *See* Petroleum

*Old age pensions

Ordinances

*Organizations
See also Clubs

P

Parades
See also Floats

Parent education

Parent-teacher associations

*Parks and reserves

Penal institutions. *See* Jails; Prisons; etc.

*Petroleum

Place names. *See* Names

Planning. *See* Beautification; City planning; etc.

*Plants
See also Flowers; Shrubs; Trees

Playgrounds

*Police

Police department

*Politics and government
See also Charter (including amendments); City officials; Congressmen; Constitution; Laws; Ordinances; name of department, etc.

Poor

*Population

Post office

Postwar problems

*Poultry raising

Power.   *See* Public utilities; etc.

*Prisons
  See also Jails

*Probation department

*Products

Public buildings.   *See* Architecture

Public library.   *See* Libraries

Public schools.   *See* Schools

Public service department

*Public utilities

*Public welfare
  See also Social welfare

*Public works
  See also Roads; etc.

*Publications
  See also Newspapers

*Publicity

Purchasing department

R

*Radio broadcasting

*Railroads

Ranches.   *See* Agriculture

*Ranchos

*Real estate
See also Building

*Recreation
See also Parks and reserves; Playgrounds; Sports and games

Red Cross

Redistricting. *See* Wards

Refuse disposal. *See* Garbage disposal; Rubbish disposal; Sewage disposal

Relief. *See* Charities

*Reports

Resources. *See* Conservation of resources; Forests and forestry; Water supply; etc.

Rest homes

Rewards, prizes, etc.

*Rivers

*Roads
See also Freeways; Streets

Rubbish disposal

S

*Safety education

*Sales tax

Salvation Army

Sanitariums. *See* Hospitals

Scholarships and fellowships

*Schools
See also Adult education; Board of education; Education; Junior colleges; Nursery schools; Universities and colleges; etc.

*Sculpture

*Seal, State

Sewage disposal

Sheriffs

*Shrubs

*Smoke prevention

Social agencies
See also Charities; Community chest; etc.

*Social conditions
See also Moral conditions; etc.

*Social planning

*Social welfare

*Soil conservation

*Sports and games

*State guard

*State hospitals

*State picnics

*Statistics

Street department

Streets

Swimming pools, Public

T

*Taxation
See also Income tax; Sales tax; etc.

Teachers

Telephones. *See* Public utilities

*Television broadcasting

*Theaters
  See also Drama; Festivals; Fiestas; etc.

*Tidelands

*Tourists

*Trade
  See also Foreign trade

Trade unions

*Traffic regulations

*Transportation

Traveler's Aid

*Trees

Trucks

U

*Unemployment

Unemployment insurance.   *See* Insurance, Unemployment

*Universities and colleges

V

Vehicle code.   *See* Motor vehicles — Laws and regulations

Veterans

Visual education.   *See* Audio-visual education

Vital statistics

Vocational education

Voters
  See also Elections

W

*Wages

Wards

Waste reclamation

*Water supply

Waterways. *See* Canals; Rivers; etc.

Weather. *See* Climate

Weather bureau

Weights and measures

Wildflowers

*Workmen's compensation

Y

Young Men's Christian Association

Young Women's Christian Association

*Youth activities

Z

Zoning

PARTIAL LIST OF ORGANIZATIONS, ETC., THAT ISSUE PAMPHLETS

For explanation of classes of organizations included, see p. 2.

For pamphlet services, books, periodicals, bibliographies, etc., see p. 3 ff.

In writing to these organizations, always ask for complete price-list of all pamphlets available, before ordering. Subjects listed (in parentheses) are indicative only of *type* of pamphlet, and are by no means comprehensive.

A listing here does not constitute a recommendation of all pamphlets issued by these organizations, as examination of *all* publications was impossible.

A

A. B. Dick Co. *See* Dick, A. B., Co.
A. J. Nystrom & Co. *See* Nystrom, A. J., & Co.
A. S. Barnes. *See* Barnes, A. S.
1. Acousticon International (Hearing)
     580 Fifth Ave., New York 19.
2. Acturial Society of America (Insurance)
     393 Seventh Ave., New York 1.
3. Adventures in Good Eating, Inc. (Hotels)
     Box 548, Bowling Green, Ky.
4. Advertising Council, Inc. (Advertising; Economics; Industry)
     25 W. 45th St., New York 19.
5. Advertising Federation of America (Advertising)
     330 W. 42d St., New York 18.
6. Aeronautical Chamber of Commerce of America (Aeronautics)
     Shoreham Bldg., 15th & H Sts., Wash. 5, D.C.

7. Aetna Life Affiliated Companies (Insurance; Safety Education
   151 Farmington Ave., Hartford 15, Conn.
8. Air Transport Association of America (Aeronautics)
   1515 Massachusetts Ave., N.W., Wash. D.C.
9. Aircraft Consulting Service (Aeronautics; Vocational Guidance)
   537 Standard Oil Bldg., Wash. 1, D.C.
10. Aircraft Industries Association, Inc. (Aeronautics)
    610 Shoreham Bldg., N.W., Wash. 5, D.C.
11. Alabama Polytechnic Institute, Agricultural Experiment Station (Agriculture)
    Auburn, Ala.
12. All-Pets (Birds; Cats; Dogs; Pets)
    P.O. Box 151, 18 Forest Ave., Fond du Lac, Wisc.
13. Allegheny Ludlum Steel Corp. (Steel)
    Brackenridge, Pa.
14. Allis-Chambers Manufacturing Co. (Safety Education)
    Box 512, Milwaukee 1, Wisc.
15. Aluminum Co. of America (Aluminum)
    801 Gulf Bldg., Pittsburgh 19, Pa.
16. Aluminum Goods Manufacturing Co. (Aluminum)
    Washington St., Manitowoc, Wisc.
17. American Abergeen-Angus Breeders Association (Cattle)
    9 Dexter Park Ave., Chicago 9, Ill.
18. American Agricultural Chemical Co. (Fertilizers)
    50 Church St., New York.
19. American Association for Adult Education (Adult Education)
    60 E. 42nd St., New York.
20. American Association of Health, Physical Education and Recreation (Games; Health; Recreation)
    1201 16th St., N.W., Wash. 6, D.C.
21. American Association of Junior Colleges (Junior Colleges)
    730 Jackson Place, Wash., D.C.
22. American Association of Medical Social Workers (Social Work)
    1834 K St., N.W., Wash. 6, D.C.

23. American Automobile Association (Motor Vehicles; Traffic Regulations)
    Pennsylvania Ave. at 17th St., Wash. 6, D.C.
24. American Aviation Publ. (Aeronautics)
    139 N. Clark St., Chicago 2, Ill.
25. American Bankers Association (Banks and Banking)
    22 E. 40th St., New York 16.
26. American Bar Association (Law; Vocational Guidance)
    1140 N. Dearborn St., Chicago, Ill.
27. American Book Publishers Council (Books and Reading)
    62 W. 47th St., New York 19.
28. American Bottlers of Carbonated Beverages (Bottles)
    1128 16th St., N.W., Wash. 6, D.C.
29. American Broadcasting Co., Public Service Division (Radio Broadcasting)
    30 Rockefeller Plaza, New York 20.
30. American Can Co., Home Economics Section (Food — Canned)
    100 Park Ave., New York 17.
31. American Cancer Society, Inc. (Cancer)
    47 Beaver St., New York 4.
32. American Ceramic Society, Inc. (Pottery; Vocational Guidance)
    2525 N. High St., Columbus 2, Ohio.
33. American Chemical Society (Chemistry; Vocational Guidance)
    1155 16th St., N.W., Wash. 6, D.C.
34. American Chicle Co. (Chewing Gum)
    30–30 Thompson Ave., Long Island City, N.Y.
35. American Crayon Co. (Art; Color)
    9 Rockefeller Plaza, New York 20.
36. American Cyanamid Co. (Chemistry)
    30 Rockefeller Plaza, New York 20.
37. American Dental Association, Council on Dental Education (Dentistry)
    222 E. Superior St., Chicago 11, Ill.
38. American Dietetic Association (Vocational Guidance)
    620 N. Michigan Ave., Chicago 11, Ill.

39. American Education Press (Fairy Tales; Science; Teaching Aids)
    400 S. Front St., Columbus, Ohio.
40. American Federation of Labor (Trade Unions)
    901 Massachusetts Ave., Wash. 1, D.C.
41. American Felt Co. (Felt)
    Glenville, Conn.
42. American Forest Products Industries (Forests and Forestry)
    1319 18th St., N.W., Wash. 6, D.C.
43. American Foundation for the Blind (Blind)
    15 W. 16th St., New York.
44. American Gas Association (Gas — Natural)
    420 Lexington Ave., New York.
45. American Geological Society (Geology)
    Broadway and 156th St., New York.
46. American Glassware Association (Glassware)
    19 W. 44th St., New York 18.
47. American Guernsey Cattle Club (Cattle)
    Peterboro, N.H.
48. American Hampshire Sheep Assoc. (Sheep)
    72 Woodland Ave., Detroit 2, Mich.
49. American Handicrafts Co. (Handicraft)
    193 William St., New York.
50. American Heart Association (Heart)
    1775 Broadway, New York 19.
51. American Home Economics Association (Food; Home Economics; Marriage)
    Mills Bldg., Wash., D.C.
52. American Hospital Association (Health; Hospitals)
    18 E. Division St., Chicago, Ill.
53. American Houses (Houses, Prefabricated)
    570 Lexington Ave., New York 12.
54. American Institute of Actuaries (Insurance)
    135 S. LaSalle St., Chicago 3, Ill.
55. American Institute of Architects (Architecture; City Planning)
    115 E. 40th St., New York 16.
56. American Institute of Baking (Food)
    1135 Fullerton Ave., Chicago 14, Ill.

57. American Institute of Family Relations (Family
    Life; Marriage)
    5287 Sunset Blvd., Los Angeles 27, Calif.
58. American Institute of Laundering (Laundry)
    Joliet, Ill.
59. American Iron and Steel Institute (Steel)
    350 Fifth Ave., New York 1.
60. American Legion (Flags; Veterans)
    777 N. Meridian St., Indianapolis, Ind.
61. American Legislator's Association (Taxation)
    1313 E. 60th St., Chicago, Ill.
62. American Library Association (Library Science)
    50 E. Huron St., Chicago 11, Ill.
63. American Management Association (Collective Bar-
    gaining; Employees; Factory Management; Indus-
    trial Relations; Management; Packaging; Produc-
    tion; Wages)
    330 W. 42nd St., New York 18.
64. American Meat Institute (Meat)
    59 E. Van Buren St., Chicago, Ill.
65. American Medical Association (Alcoholism; Health;
    Hospitals; Nutrition; Occupational Therapy; Vita-
    mins)
    535 N. Dearborn St., Chicago 10, Ill.
66. American Meteorite Museum (Meteors)
    Winslow, Ariz.
67. American Municipal Association (Municipal Gov-
    ernment)
    1313 E. 60th St., Chicago 37, Ill.
68. American Museum of Natural History (Animals;
    Birds; Nature; Science)
    Central Park West at 79th St., New York.
69. American Nature Association (Animals; Birds;
    Fishes; Flowers; Herbs; Insects; Reptiles; Spi-
    ders; Weeds)
    1214 16th St., N.W., Wash. 6, D.C.
70. American Nurses' Association, Nursing Information
    Bureau (Nurses and Nursing)
    1790 Broadway, New York 19.

71. American Optical Co., Scientific Instrument Division (Microscopy)
Buffalo 15, N.Y.

72. American Optometric Association (Optometry)
Jenkins Bldg., Pittsburgh 22, Pa.

73. American Osteopathic Association (Osteopathy)
212 E. Ohio St., Chicago 11, Ill.

74. American Petroleum Institute (Petroleum)
50 W. 50th St., New York 20.

75. American Power Boat Association (Boats and Boating)
American Security Bldg., Wash., D.C.

76. American Prison Association (Crime and Criminals; Prisons)
135 E. 15th St., New York.

77. American Public Health Association (Nurses and Nursing; Nutrition; Public Health; Swimming Pools)
1790 Broadway, New York 19.

78. American (National) Red Cross (Disasters; First Aid in Illness and Injury; Red Cross)
17th and E. Sts., N.W., Wash. 13, D.C.

79. American Reedcraft Corp. (Handicraft)
83 Beekman St., New York 7.

80. American Social Hygiene Association (Health; Sex Hygiene; Social Hygiene)
1790 Broadway, New York 19.

81. American Society for the Hard of Hearing (Deaf)
1537 35th St., N.W., Wash., D.C.

82. American Society of Agricultural Engineers (Agricultural Engineering)
505 Pleasant St., Saint Joseph, Mich.

83. American Society of Composers, Authors and Publishers (Songs)
30 Rockefeller Plaza, New York 20.

84. American Society of Planning Officials (Automobile Parking; City Planning)
1313 E. 60th St., Chicago 37, Ill.

85. American Spice Trade Association (Spices)
82 Wall St., New York 5.

86. American Standards Association (Electric Apparatus
and Appliances; Standardization)
29 W. 39th St., New York 18.

87. American Steel and Wire Co., Advertising Dept.
(Wire)
Rockefeller Bldg., Cleveland, Ohio.

88. American Sugar Refining Co. (Sugar)
120 Wall St., New York 5.

89. American Taxpayers Association (Taxation)
Munsey Bldg., Wash. 4, D.C.

90. American Technical Society (Aerodynamics)
850 E. 58th St., Chicago, Ill.

91. American Thread Co., Inc. (Cotton; Thread)
260 W. Broadway, New York.

92. American Trucking Association (Motor Trucks)
1424 16th St., N.W., Wash. 6, D.C.

93. American Viscose Co., Consumer Service (Silk, Artificial Textiles)
350 Fifth Ave., New York 1.

94. American Walnut Manufacturers Association (Furniture)
616 S. Michigan Blvd., Chicago, Ill.

95. American Wool Council, Inc. (Knitting; Wool)
1450 Broadway, New York 18.

96. American Zinc Institute (Zinc)
60 E. 42nd St., New York.

97. Anaconda Copper Mining Co. (Copper)
25 Broadway, New York 4.

98. Ansco (Photography)
247 E. Ontario St., Chicago, Ill.

99. Anthracite Institute (Coal)
101 Park Ave., New York 17.

100. Appalachian Hardwood Manufacturers, Inc. (Lumber)
44 Walnut St., Cincinnati, Ohio.

101. Archway Press (Beauty, Personal; Etiquette;
Home)
41 W. 47th St., New York 19.

102. Arkansas Soft Pine Bureau (Building; Lumber)
Boyle Bldg., Little Rock, Ark.

103. Arkansas University, College of Agriculture (Agriculture; Home Economics)
     Little Rock, Arkansas.
104. Armour and Co. (Meat)
     U.S. Yards, Chicago, Ill.
105. Armstrong Cork Co., Floor Division (Floor Coverings)
     Lancaster, Pa.
106. Art Handicrafts Leather Co. (Handicraft; Leather Work)
     26 Frankfort St., New York.
107. Arts Cooperative Service (Art; Handicraft; Units of Work)
     340 Amsterdam Ave., New York 24.
108. Asphalt Institute (Asphalt; Roads)
     801 Second Ave., New York 17.
109. Associated Aviation Underwriters (Aeronautics)
     90 John St., New York 7.
110. Association for Childhood Education (Child Study; Nursery Schools; Kindergarten-Primary Education)
     1201 16th St., N.W., Wash. 6, D.C.
111. Association of American Playing Card Manufacturers (Cards)
     420 Lexington Ave., New York 17.
112. Association of American Railroads (Railroads)
     Transportation Bldg., Wash. 6, D.C.
113. Association of Casualty and Surety Companies, Accident Prevention Dept. (Accidents — Prevention of)
     60 John St., New York.
114. Association of National Advertisers (Advertising)
     330 W. 42nd St., New York 18.
115. Atchison, Topeka and Santa Fe Railway System (Railroads)
     80 E. Jackson Blvd., Chicago 4, Ill.
116. Author and Journalist (Writing)
     1759 S. Pearl St., Denver 10, Colo.
117. Automobile Manufacturers Association (Automobile Industry; Automobiles)
     320 New Center Bldg., Detroit 2, Mich.

118. Axe, E. W. & Co. (Agricultural Machinery)
730 Fifth Ave., New York.

B

1. Baker, Walter H., Co. (Dramas)
178 Tremont St., Boston 11, Mass.
2. Ball Brothers Co. (Canning and Preserving)
Muncie, Ind.
B. F. Goodrich Co. *See* Goodrich, B. F., Co.
3. Bantam Books, Inc. (General)
1223 Public Ledger Bldg., Philadelphia 6, Pa.
4. Barnes, A. S. (General; Sports)
100 Fifth Ave., New York.
5. Bausch & Lamb Optical Co. (Microscopy)
635 St. Paul St., Rochester 2, New York.
6. Becton, Dickinson & Co. (First Aid in Illness and Injury)
Rutherford, N.J.
7. Beech Aircraft Corp. (Aeronautics)
Wichita, Kans.
8. Beech-Nut Packing Co. (Chewing-Gum)
Canajoharie, N.Y.
9. Behr-Manning Corp. (Machinery; Tools)
Troy, N.Y.
10. Belgian Draft Horse Corp. of America (Horses)
Wabash, Ind.
11. Bell Telephone & Telegraph System (Biography;
Telephone)
195 Broadway, New York.
12. Bellman Publishing Co., Inc. (Industry; Vocational
Guidance)
83 Newbury St., Boston 16, Mass.
13. Berks Printing Co. (Chinchillas)
Reading, Pa.
14. Bernhard Ulmann Co. (Knitting; Yarn)
30–20 Thomson Ave., Long Island City 1, New York.
15. Berrien Bindery (Geography; Nature; Travel; Units
of Work)
Berrien Springs, Mich.

16. Bethlehem Steel Corp. (Steel)
    Bethlehem, Pa.
17. Better Vision Institute (Eye)
    3157 International Bldg., Rockefeller Center, New York 20.
18. Bibb Manufacturing Co. (Cotton)
    Macon, Georgia.
19. Bicycle Institute of America. (Cycling)
    122 E. 42nd St., New York.
20. Bigelow-Sanford Carpet Co., Home Service Bureau (Floor Coverings; Interior Decoration)
    140 Madison Ave., New York 16.
21. Binney & Smith Co. (Art)
    42 E. 42nd St., New York 17.
22. Bituminous Coal Institute (Air Pollution; Coal; Smoke Prevention)
    Southern Bldg., Wash. 5, D.C.
23. Bohr-Manning, Division of Norton Co. (Abrasives)
    Troy, New York.
24. Borden Co. (Food; Health; Milk, Evaporated)
    350 Madison Ave., New York 17.
25. Boston Better Business Bureau (Advertising; Better Business Bureaus)
    52 Chauncy St., Boston, Mass.
26. Boston University, School & College Relations (Vocational Guidance)
    705 Commonwealth Ave., Boston 15, Mass.
27. Botany Mills (Wool)
    16 W. 46th St., New York 19.
28. Botany Worsted Millers (Wool)
    Pasaic, N.J.
29. Boucher Ship Models Co. (Ships — Models)
    36 E. 12th St., New York.
30. Bowker, R. R. Co. (Books and Reading)
    62 W. 45th St., New York 19.
31. Boy Scouts of America (Boy Scouts; Hobbies)
    2 Park Ave., New York 16.
32. Boys' Clubs of America (Boys; Boys' Clubs)
    381 Fourth Ave., New York 16.

33. Bristol-Myers Co., Educational Service Dept. (Beauty, Personal; Dentistry)
630 Fifth Ave., New York 20.

34. Broadcast Measurement Bureau Inc. (Radio Broadcasting)
270 Park Ave., New York 17.

35. Brooklyn Botanical Garden (Botany; Herbs)
1000 Washington Ave., Brooklyn, N.Y.

36. Brooklyn Museum, The Brooklyn Institute of Arts & Sciences (Art; Textiles)
Brooklyn, N.Y.

37. Buescher Band Instrument Co., (Music; Musical Instruments)
Elkhart, Ind.

38. Bureau of Coffee Information (Coffee)
230 Park Ave., New York.

39. Burgess Handicraft & Hobby Service (Handicraft; Hobbies)
117 N. Wabash Ave., Chicago, Ill.

40. Burlington Mills Corp. of N.Y. (Textiles)
26 W. 40th St., New York.

41. Burnett, Joseph, Co. (Food)
Boston 10, Mass.

42. Burroughs Adding Machine Co. (Business Machines; Mathematics)
Detroit 32, Mich.

43. Business Week (Business)
330 W. 42nd St., New York 18.

C

C. G. Conn, Ltd. *See* Conn, C. G., Ltd.
C. S. Hammond & Co. *See* Hammond, C. S. & Co.

1. California & Hawaiian Sugar Refining Corp., Ltd. (Sugar)
215 Market St., San Francisco, Calif.

2. California Foods Research Institute (Food; Fruit)
1 Drumm St., San Francisco 11, Calif.

3. California Fruit Growers Exchange (Fruit; Nutrition)
Box 5030, Los Angeles 54, Calif.

4. California Olive Association (Olives)
   461 Market St., San Francisco 5, Calif.
5. California Redwood Association (Lumber)
   405 Montgomery St., San Francisco 4, Calif.
6. California State Department of Education (Vocational Guidance)
   Sacramento, Calif.
7. Cambridge Glass Co. (Glassware)
   Cambridge, Ohio.
8. Cambridge University Press (Printing; Writing)
   32 E. 57th St., New York 52.
9. Cannon Mills, Inc. (Linen — Household)
   70 Worth St., New York.
10. Carpet Institute, Inc. (Floor Coverings)
    350 Fifth Ave., New York 1.
11. Carrier Corporation (Air Conditioning)
    Syracuse, N.Y.
12. Case, J. I., Co., Inc. (Agricultural Machinery; Agriculture; Conservation of Resources)
    Racine, Wisc.
13. Cast Iron Pipe Research Assoc. (Water-Supply)
    122 S. Michigan Ave., Chicago, Ill.
14. Catalin Corporation of America (Plastics)
    1 Park Ave., New York 16.
15. Caterpillar Tractor Co. (Forests and Forestry)
    Peoria 8, Ill.
16. Catholic Library Association (Catholic Literature)
    P. O. Box 25, Kingsbridge Station, New York 63.
17. Celanese Corporation of America (Home Economics; Silk, Artificial; Textiles)
    180 Madison Ave., New York 16.
18. Cereal Institute, Inc. (Cereals; Nutrition)
    135 S. LaSalle St., Chicago 3, Ill.
19. Chamber of Commerce of the U.S. (Agriculture; Business; Economics; Political Science; Socialism; Unemployment; Veterans; Welfare State)
    1615 H St., N.W., Wash. 6, D.C.
20. Chambers Corporation (Cookery)
    Shelbyville, Ind.
    Charles E. Merrill Co. *See* Merrill, Charles E., Co.

21. Chase National Bank (Money)
    Pine St. at Nassau St., New York 15.
22. Chicago Natural History Museum (Anthropology;
    Birds; Botany; Geology; Mineralogy; Nature; Science; Zoology)
    Roosevelt Road & Lake Shore Drive, Chicago 5,
    Ill.
23. Chicago Tribune (General)
    Tribune Tower, Chicago, Ill.
24. Child Study Association of America (Child Study)
    221 W. 57th St., New York 19.
25. Children's Book Council (Children's Literature)
    62 W. 45th St., New York 19.
26. Cleanliness Institute (Hygiene)
    295 Madison Ave., New York 17.
27. Clemson College, Extension Service (DDT; Insects)
    Clemson, S.C.
28. Clinton Carpet Co. (Floor Coverings)
    Merchandise Mart, Chicago, Ill.
29. Cluett, Peabody & Co., Inc. (Advertising; Clothing &
    Dress)
    10 E. 40th St., New York.
30. Colgate-Palmolive-Peet Co. (Soap)
    105 Hudson, Jersey City 2, N.J.
31. Colonial Williamsburg (Colonial Life and Customs;
    Williamsburg, Va.)
    Williamsburg, Va.
32. Colorado Agricultural College (Agriculture; Home
    Economics)
    Fort Collins, Colo.
33. Columbian Rope Co. (Rope)
    Auburn, N.Y.
34. Committee for Constitutional Government, Inc. (United
    States — Constitution)
    205 E. 42nd St., New York 17.
35. Committee for the Nation's Health (Health)
    1416 F St., N.W., Wash., D.C.
36. Committee on Consumer Relations in Advertising, Inc.
    (Advertising; Consumer Education)
    420 Lexington Ave., New York 17.

37. Common Council for American Unity (Subversive Activities)
    20 W. 40th St., New York 18.
38. Commonwealth Club of California (Water Supply)
    Hotel St. Francis, San Francisco 19, Calif.
39. Community Chests and Councils (Community Chests; Social Work)
    155 E. 44th St., New York 17.
40. Compton, F. E., and Co. Department of Library Service (Encyclopedias; General; Teaching Aids)
    1000 N. Dearborn St., Chicago 10, Ill.
41. Congress of Industrial Organizations (Trade Unions)
    718 Jackson Place, N.W., Wash. 6, D.C.
42. Conn, C. G., Ltd. (Music; Musical Instruments)
    Elkhart, Ind.
43. Consumer Education Study (Consumer Education)
    1201 16th St., N.W., Wash. 6, D.C.
44. Cooperative Recreation Service (Recreation)
    Delaware, Ohio.
45. Copper & Brass Research Association (Agricultural Machinery; Copper)
    420 Lexington Ave., New York 17.
46. Corn Industries Research Foundation (Corn)
    3 E. 45th St., New York 17.
47. Cornell University, New York State College of Agriculture (Agriculture; Home Economics)
    Ithaca, N.Y.
48. Corning Glass Works (Chemistry; Glassware)
    Corning, N.Y.
49. Council of State Governments (State Governments)
    1313 E. 60th St., Chicago 37, Ill.
50. Council on Candy of the National Confectioners' Association (Candy; Food)
    1 N. LaSalle St., Chicago 2, Ill.
51. Cram, George F., Co., Inc. (Teaching Aids)
    Indianapolis 7, Ind.
52. Cranbrook Institute of Science (Birds; Science)
    Bloomfield Hills, Mich.
53. Crowell-Collier Publishing Co. (Health)
    250 Park Ave., New York 17.

54. Crown Zellerbach Corporation (Paper Making and Trade)

Rincon Annex, Box 3475, San Francisco, Calif.

55. Curtiss Wright Corporation (Aeronautics)

30 Rockefeller Plaza, New York 20.

D

1. Dan River Mills, Inc. (Textiles)

40 Worth St., New York 13.

2. Delco Appliances Division, General Motors Sales Corporation (Fuel)

Rochester, N.Y.

3. Delta Power Tool Division, Rockwell Manufacturing Co. (Tools; Woodworking)

Milwaukee, Wisc.

4. Demco Library Supplies (Bookbinding; Libraries — Supplies)

Madison, Wisc.

5. Denlinger's (Aquariums)

Wash., D.C.

6. Dennison Manufacturing Co. (Costume; Entertaining; Handicraft)

Framingham, Mass.

7. Denoyer-Geppert Co. (Maps)

5235 Ravenswood Ave., Chicago 40, Ill.

8. Denver Art Museum (Art; Indians of North America)

1300 Logan St., Denver, Colo.

9. Denver Museum of Natural History (Mineralogy)

City Park, Denver, Colo.

10. Diamond Match Co. (Matches)

475 Fifth Ave., New York.

11. Dick, A. B., Co. (Mimeographing)

5700 W. Touhy Ave., Chicago 31, Ill.

12. Diesel Publishers (Diesel Engines)

192 Lexington Ave., New York 16.

13. Disston, Henry, & Sons, Inc. (Tools)

Unruh & Milnor, Philadelphia, Pa.

14. Division of Information, Dept. of Conservation (Conservation of Resources)

Nashville, Tenn.

15. Division of University Extension, Knoxville (Consumer Education)
    Box 4218, University Station, Knoxville, Tenn.
16. Douglas Fir Plywood Association (Lumber)
    1707 Daily News Bldg., Chicago 6, Ill.
17. Dramatists Play Service (Dramas)
    14 E. 38th St., New York 16.
18. Drexel Institute of Technology, Public Relations Dept. (Library Science)
    32nd & Chestnut Sts., Philadelphia 4, Pa.
19. Dritz, John, & Sons (Sewing)
    1115 Broadway, New York 10.
20. Dun and Bradstreet (Credit)
    290 Broadway, New York 8.
21. DuPont, E. I., de Nemours Co. (Furniture; "Miracle Fabrics"; Silk, Artificial; Textiles)
    Wilmington 98, Del.
22. Dwinnell-Wright Co. (Teaching Aids)
    68 Fargo St., Boston, Mass.

E

E. I. DuPont de Nemours Co. *See* DuPont, E. I. de Nemours Co.
1. Eastman Kodak Co. (Photography)
   Rochester 4, N.Y.
2. Easy Washing Machine Corporation (Laundry)
   Syracuse, N.Y.
3. Edison General Electric Appliance Co., Inc. (Electric Apparatus & Appliances)
   5611 W. Taylor St., Chicago, Ill.
4. Educational Research Bureau (General; Teaching Aids)
   1217 13th St., N.W., Wash., D.C.
5. Electric Storage Battery Co. (Batteries; Weather)
   Allegheny Ave. & 19th St., Philadelphia 32, Pa.
6. Emergency Conservation Committee (Birds)
   734 Lexington Ave., New York.
7. Empire State Bldg. (Buildings)
   350 Fifth Ave., New York 1

8. Encyclopaedia Britannica (Encyclopedias; General)
   283 Madison Ave., New York.
9. Engineers Council for Professional Development (Engineering Education)
   29 W. 39th St., New York 18.
10. Enoch Pratt Free Library (Books and Reading)
   Cathedral & Mulberry Sts., Baltimore 1, Md.
11. Esto Publishing Co. (Art)
   P. O. Box 46M, Pasadena 16, Calif.
12. Evaporated Milk Association (Cookery; Milk, Evaporated)
   307 Michigan Ave., Chicago, Ill.

F

F. E. Compton & Co. *See* Compton, F. E., & Co.
F. W. Faxon Co. *See* Faxon, F. W., Co.
1. Family Life Institute, University of Oklahoma (Family Life; Parent Education)
   North Campus, University of Oklahoma, Norman, Okla.
2. Farmers & Manufacturers Beet Sugar Association (Sugar)
   2d National Bank Bldg., Saginaw 5, Mich.
3. Faxon, F. W., Co. (Library Science)
   83 Francis St., Back Bay, Boston, Mass.
4. Federal Reserve Bank of Minneapolis (Money)
   Minneapolis, Minn.
5. Fellowcrafters, Inc. (Handicraft; Leather Work)
   18 Oliver St., Boston, Mass.
6. Fels & Co. (Soap)
   73d & Woodland Ave., Philadelphia 42, Pa.
7. Field Enterprises Inc., Educational Division (Encyclopedias; General)
   Reference Library, 35 W. Wacker Drive, Chicago 1, Ill.
8. Firestone Tire & Rubber Co. (Rubber)
   Akron 17, Ohio.
9. Firth Carpet Co. (Floor Coverings)
   295 5th Ave., New York 16.

10. Fisher Scientific Co. (Accidents — Prevention of)
    711–723 Forbes St., Pittsburgh, Pa.
11. Fleer, Frank H., Corporation (Chewing Gum)
    10th & Somerville, Philadelphia 41, Pa.
12. Fleisher Yarns, Inc. (Yarn)
    30–20 Thomson Ave., Long Island City 1, New York.
13. Florida Dept. of Agriculture (Agriculture; Home
    Economics)
    Tallahassee, Fla.
14. Fogg Museum of Art (Art)
    Cambridge, Mass.
15. Foley-Tripp Co. (Handicraft)
    193 William St., New York.
16. Food Research Institute (Agriculture; Food)
    Stanford University, Calif.
17. Forestry Enterprises (Forests and Forestry)
    1740 K St., N.W., Wash., D.C.
18. Fostoria Glass Co. (Glassware)
    Moundsville, W. Va.
19. Foundation for Economic Education (Economics)
    Irvington-on-Hudson, New York.
    Frank H. Fleer Corporation. *See* Fleer, Frank H.,
    Corporation
20. French, Samuel, Inc. (Dramas)
    25 W. 45 St., New York 19.
21. Friedman-Shelby Division, International Shoe Co.
    (Shoes)
    1507 Washington Ave., St. Louis 3, Mo.
22. Fruit Dispatch Co. (Fruit)
    Pier 3, North River, New York 6.
23. Funk & Wagnalls Co. (Words)
    153 E. 24th St., New York 10.

G

G. Schirmer, Inc. *See* Schirmer, G., Inc.
G. & C. Merriam Co. *See* Merriam Co., G. & C.
1. Gale, Dr. Louis Clyde (Animals)
    P.O. Box 451, Concordia, Kans.

2. Garden Club of America (Flowers; Gardens)
598 Madison Ave., New York 22.

3. Gaylord Bros. (Bookbinding; Libraries — Supplies)
155 Gifford St., Syracuse 1, N.Y.

4. General Aniline & Film Corporation (Photography)
Binghamton, N.Y.

5. General Biological Supply House (Biology; Hobbies; Science)
761–763 E. 69th Place, Chicago 37, Ill.

6. General Electric Home Service Institute (Cookery; Food)
Bridgeport, Conn.

7. General Mills, Inc., Education Section (Consumer Education; Nutrition)
400 Second Ave., S., Minneapolis 1, Minn.

8. General Motors Corporation (Automobiles; Tools)
General Motors Bldg., 3044 Grand Blvd., Detroit 2, Mich.
George F. Cram Co. *See* Cram, George F., Co., Inc.

9. Georgia Marble Co. (Marble)
Tate, Ga.

10. Georgia State College of Agriculture (Agriculture; Home Economics)
Athens, Ga.

11. Gerber Products Co. (Child Study)
Fremont, Mich.

12. Girl Scouts of the U.S.A. (Girl Scouts; Hobbies; Nature; Vocational Guidance)
155 E. 44th St., New York.

13. Glamour Magazine, Job Dept. (Vocational Guidance)
420 Lexington Ave., New York 17.

14. Good Housekeeping (Accidents — Prevention of; Home Economics; Interior Decoration; Laundry)
959 Eighth Ave., New York 19.

15. Goodrich, B. F., Co. (Aeronautics; Rubber)
Akron, Ohio.

16. Goodyear Aircraft Corporation (Aeronautics)
Akron, Ohio.

17. Goodyear Tire & Rubber Co. (Rubber)
Akron, Ohio.

18. Gorham Co. (Silverware; Table)
   Providence 7, R.I.
19. Gorton-Pew Fisheries Co. (Cookery; Fish [as Food])
   Gloucester, Mass.
20. Gray Marine Motor Co. (Marine Engines)
   6910 E. Lafayette Ave., Detroit, Mich.
21. Grosset and Dunlap (General; Vocational Guidance)
   1107 Broadway, New York 10.
22. Gruen Watch Co. (Clocks and Watches)
   Cincinnati 6, Ohio.
23. Gulf Oil Corporation (Sugar)
   Gulf Bldg., Pittsburgh, Pa.

H

H. J. Heinz Co. *See* Heinz, H. J., Co.
H. W. Wilson Co. *See* Wilson, H. W., Co.
1. Hammond, C. S., & Co. (Geography; Maps)
   305 E. 63d St., New York 21.
2. Handcrafters (Handicraft)
   Waupin, Wisc.
3. Handy & Harman (Handicraft; Silver)
   82 Fulton St., New York.
4. Harian Publications (Travel)
   Greenlawn, N.Y.
5. Harmon Foundation (Negroes)
   140 Nassau St., New York.
6. Hart, Lawrence H. (Encyclopedias)
   14 W. Walnut St., Metuchen, N.J.
7. Hayden Planetarium (Astronomy)
   81st St. near Central Park W., New York 24.
8. Health Publications Institute, Inc. (Child Study;
   Health; Venereal Diseases)
   216 N. Dawson St., Raleigh, N.C.
9. Heinz, H. J., Co. (Food — Canned)
   Pittsburgh, Pa.
   Henry Disston & Sons, Inc. *See* Disston, Henry &
   Sons, Inc.
10. Hercules Powder Co. (Paper Making and Trade)
   Wilmington 99, Del.

11. Hershey Chocolate Corporation (Cocoa and Chocolate)
    Hershey, Pa.
12. Higgins Ink Co., Inc. (Art)
    271 Ninth St., Brooklyn 15, N.Y.
13. Highway Research Board (Roads)
    2101 Constitution Ave., Wash. 25, D.C.
14. Hillsway Co. (Hotels; Travel)
    1620 E. 2d St., Long Beach, Calif.
15. Holstein-Friesian Association of America (Cattle)
    1 South Main St., Brattleboro, Vt.
16. Home Institute (General; Hobbies; Vocational Guidance)
    109 W. 19th St., New York.
17. Home Workshop Library, General Pub. Co., Inc., (Carpentry; Woodworking) 154 E. Erie, Chicago, Ill.
18. Homecrafts Publishers (Beauty, Personal; Handicraft; Hats)
    799 Broadway, New York 3.
19. Hoover Co. (Electric Apparatus and Appliances; Home Economics)
    North Canton, Ohio.
20. Household Finance Corporation (Consumer Education)
    919 N. Michigan Ave., Chicago 11, Ill.
21. Hudson Coal Co. (Coal)
    424 Wyoming Ave., Scranton 1, Pa.

I

1. Imperial Paper and Color Corporation (Wall Coverings)
   Glens Falls, N.Y.
2. Institute for Research in the Professions and Vocations (Vocational Guidance)
   537 S. Dearborn St., Chicago, Ill.
3. Institute of Life Insurance (Budget — Household; Insurance; Marriage)
   488 Madison Ave., New York 22

4. Institute of Traffic Engineers (Traffic Regulations)
   60 John St., New York 7.
5. International City Manager's Association (Municipal Government)
   1313 E. 60th St., Chicago, Ill.
6. International Harvester Co. (Agricultural Machinery; Electric Apparatus and Appliances)
   180 N. Michigan Ave., Chicago 1, Ill.
7. International Nickel Co., Inc. (Nickel)
   67 Wall St., New York 5.
8. International Salt Co. (Salt)
   Scranton, Pa.
   International Shoe Co. *See* Friedman-Shelby Division
9. International Silk Guild (Silk)
   250 Fifth Ave., New York.
10. Interstate Printers & Publishers (Child Study)
    19–27 N. Jackson St., Danville, Ill.
11. Iowa State College of Agriculture & Mechanical Arts (Agriculture; Home Economics)
    Ames, Iowa.
12. Irish Linen Guild (Linen — Household)
    1270 Ave. of the Americas, New York 20.
13. Irwin-Harrisons-Whitney, Inc. (Tea)
    111 N. Canal St., Chicago 6, Ill.
14. Isaak Walton League of America, Inc. (Conservation of Resources)
    31 N. State St., Chicago 2, Ill.

J

J. I. Case Co., Inc. *See* Case, J. I., Co.
John Dritz and Sons. *See* Dritz, John, & Sons
1. John Hancock Mutual Life Insurance Co. (Health; Insurance)
   Boston, Mass.
   Joseph Burnett Co. *See* Burnett, Joseph, & Co.
2. Judy Publishing Co. (Dogs)
   3323 Michigan Blvd., Chicago 16, Ill.

K

1. Kansas State College, School of Home Economics
   (Cookery; Home Economics)
   Manhattan, Kans.
2. Kellogg's, Home Economics Dept. (Nutrition)
   Battle Creek, Mich.
3. Kentucky University, College of Agriculture (Agriculture; Home Economics)
   Lexington, Ky.
4. Kerr Glass Manufacturing Corporation (Canning and
   Preserving)
   2912 Title Insurance Bldg., Los Angeles, Calif.
5. Keyboard Jr. (Music; Musical Instruments)
   1346 Chapel St., New Haven, Conn.
6. Kimberly-Clark Corporation (Home)
   Neenah, Wisc.
7. Klearflax Linen Looms, Inc. (Linen — Household)
   Duluth, Minn.
8. Klipto Loose Leaf Co. (Science; Teaching Aids)
   Mason City, Iowa.
9. Kraft Foods Co. (Cheese)
   500 Peshtigo Court, Chicago, Ill.

L

1. L. C. Smith and Corona Typewriter, Inc. (Typewriting)
   701 E. Washington St., Syracuse 1, N.Y.
2. Lake Superior Mink Farm (Animals)
   2605 E. 7th St., Superior, Wisc.
3. Lamont, Corliss & Co. (Cocoa and Chocolate)
   577 E. Illinois St., Chicago, Ill.
4. Lane Publishing Co. (Home)
   Menlo Park, Calif.
5. Lead Industries Association (Lead)
   420 Lexington Ave., New York 17.
6. Lehigh Navigation Coal Co. (Coal)
   Fidelity-Philadelphia Trust Bldg., Philadelphia 9,
   Pa.

7. Lehn and Fink Products Corporation (Home)
   Bloomfield, N.J.
8. Leisure League of America, Sentinel Books (Hobbies)
   112 E. 19th St., New York.
9. LePage's, Inc. (Glue)
   Gloucester, Mass.
10. Lever Brothers Co. (Nutrition; Soap)
    390 Park Ave., New York.
11. Life Insurance Agency Management Association (Insurance)
    115 Broad St., Hartford 5, Conn.
12. Life Insurance Association of America (Insurance)
    165 Broadway, New York 6.
13. Lincoln National Life Insurance Co. (Insurance; Lincoln, Abraham)
    Fort Wayne, Ind.
14. Lorenz Publishing Co. (General; Holidays)
    504 E. 3d St., Dayton 1, Ohio.
15. Louisiana Dept. of Education (Teaching Aids)
    Baton Rouge 4, La.
16. Louisiana State Dept. of Agriculture and Immigration (Cotton; Rice; Sugar)
    P.O. Box 951, Baton Rouge, La.
17. Louisiana State University Library School (Library Science)
    Baton Rouge 3, La.

M

1. McCormick & Co. (Spices; Tea)
   Light & Barre, Baltimore 2, Md.
2. McIntire Co., Publishers (Hats)
   5225 Wilshire Blvd., Los Angeles 36, Calif.
3. McKinley Publishing Co. (History; Maps)
   809–811 N. 19th St., Philadelphia, Pa.
4. McKnight & McKnight (Astronomy)
   Bloomington, Ill.
5. Mademoiselle (Vocational Guidance)
   133 E. 42d St., New York 17.

6. Mahogany Association, Inc. (Lumber)
   75 E. Wacker Dr., Chicago 1, Ill.
7. Maine University, College of Agriculture (Agriculture; Home Economics)
   Orono, Maine.
8. Mallenckrodt Chemical Works (Chemistry)
   St. Louis 7, Mo.
9. Mandeville & King Co. (Flowers)
   Rochester, N.Y.
10. Manual Arts Press (Carpentry; Woodworking)
    Peoria, Ill.
11. Marketing Research Service (Teaching Aids)
    2300 Conn. Ave., Wash. 8, D.C.
12. Martin Memorial Library (Pennsylvania)
    York, Pa.
13. Maryland University (Home Economics)
    College Park, Md.
14. Massachusetts Horticultural Society (Herbs; Plants)
    Horticultural Hall, Boston 15, Mass.
15. Maternity Center Association (Maternity Welfare)
    370 Seventh Ave., New York.
16. Meredith Publishing Co. (Cookery; Home)
    1716 Locust St., Des Moines 3, Iowa.
17. Merriam, G. & C., Co. (Words)
    Springfield, Mass.
18. Merrill, Charles E., Co. (Teaching Aids)
    Columbus 15, Ohio.
19. Metropolitan Life Insurance Co. (Accidents — Prevention of; Health; Insurance; Safety Education)
    1 Madison Ave., New York 10.
20. Michigan State College (Agricultural Machinery; Agriculture; Fertilizers; Home Economics)
    Extension Division, East Lansing, Mich.
21. Michigan State Employment Service (Vocational Guidance)
    7310 Woodward Ave., Detroit 2, Mich.
22. Milbank Memorial Fund (Nutrition)
    40 Wall St., New York 5.
23. Milk Foundation (Milk; Scientists)
    28 E. Huron St., Chicago 11, Ill.

24. Millers' National Federation (Grain Trade)
      309 W. Jackson Blvd., Chicago 6, Ill.
25. Milwaukee Journal (Journalism)
      Milwaukee, Wisc.
26. Mississippi Agricultural and Mechanical College (Agriculture; Home Economics)
      A. & M. College (Station), Miss.
27. Missouri University (Home Economics)
      Columbia, Mo.
28. Monroe Chemical Co. (Color; Dyes and Dyeing)
      3d and Oak Sts., Quincy, Ill.
29. Montana State College (Home Economics)
      Bozeman, Mont.
30. More Game Birds in America, a Foundation (Birds)
      500 Fifth Ave., New York.
31. Morton Salt Co. (Salt)
      120 S. LaSalle St., Chicago 3, Ill.
32. Mossberg, O. F. (Guns; Sports)
      New Haven 5, Conn.
33. Motion Picture Association of America (Moving Pictures)
      28 W. 44th St., New York 18.
34. Municipal Finance Officers Association (Accounting)
      1313 E. 60th St., Chicago 37, Ill.
35. Municipal Reference Library, New York (Budget — Municipal)
      Municipal Bldg., New York 7.

N

1. National Aeronautics Council (Aeronautics)
      37 W. 47th St., New York.
2. National Association of Better Business Bureaus (Better Business Bureaus)
      Cuyahoga Rd., Cleveland 14, Ohio.
3. National Association of Broadcasters (Radio Broadcasting)
      1760 N. St., N.W., Wash., D.C.
4. National Association of Ice Industries (Ice)
      1716 L. St., N.W., Wash., D.C.

5. National Association of Manufacturers (Business; Corporations; Industrial Relations; Inventions; Manufactures; Teaching Aids)
   14 W. 49th St., New York.

6. National Association of Margarine Manufacturers (Oleomargarine)
   Munsey Bldg., Wash. 4, D.C.

7. National Association of the Flour Milling Industry (Bread)
   309 W. Jackson Blvd., Chicago 6, Ill.

8. National Association of Wool Manufacturers (Wool)
   386 Fourth Ave., New York 16.

9. National Audubon Society (Birds; Nature)
   1000 5th Ave., New York 28.

10. National Better Business Bureau, Inc. (Better Business Bureaus)
    Chrysler Bldg., 405 Lexington Ave., New York 17.

11. National Board of Fire Underwriters (Fire Protection)
    85 John St., New York.

12. National Board of Review of Motion Pictures (Moving Pictures)
    70 Fifth Ave., New York.

13. National Canners Association (Cookery; Food — Canned)
    1739 H St., N.W., Wash., D.C.

14. National Cash Register Co. (Salesmen and Salesmanship)
    Main & K Sts., Dayton 9, Ohio.

15. National Cement Association (Airports)
    33 W. Grand Ave., Chicago, Ill.

16. National Chinchilla Breeders of America, Inc. (Chinchillas)
    P.O. Box 1806, Salt Lake City 12, Utah.

17. National Coal Association (Coal)
    Southern Bldg., Wash., D.C.

18. National Congress of Parents and Teachers (Parent-Teacher Associations)
    1201 16th St., N.W., Wash. 6, D.C.

19. National Consumer-Retailer Council (Consumer Education)
1860 Broadway, New York 23.

20. National Consumer's League (Consumer Education)
156 5th Ave., New York.

21. National Cotton Council of America (Cotton)
Box 18, Memphis 1, Tenn.

22. National Cottonseed Products Association (Cottonseed)
Memphis, Tenn.

23. National Dairy Council (Dairying; Health)
111 Canal St., Chicago 6, Ill.

24. National Dog Welfare Guild (Dogs)
114 E. 32d St., New York 16.

25. National Electrical Manufacturers Association (Electric Apparatus and Appliances)
155 E. 44th St., New York 17.

26. National Federation of American Shipping, Inc. (Shipping)
1809 G St., N.W., Wash. 6, D.C.

27. National Federation of Music Clubs (Music)
320 Wait Ave., Ithaca, New York.

28. National Federation of Textiles (Silk, Artificial; Textiles)
289 5th Ave., New York 16.

29. National Fertilizer Association, Inc. (Fertilizers)
616 Investment Bldg., Wash., D.C.

30. National Fire Protection Association (Fire Protection)
60 Batterymarch St., Boston 10, Mass.

31. National Foremen's Institute (Safety Education)
Deep River, Conn.

32. National Foundation for Infantile Paralysis (Infantile Paralysis)
120 Broadway, New York 5.

33. National Garden Bureau (Gardens)
407 S. Dearborn St., Chicago 5, Ill.

34. National Geographic Society (Geography; Nature; Travel)
School Service Dept., 16th & M Sts., Wash. 6, D.C.

35. National Highway Users Conference (Highway Transportation; Motor Vehicles)
National Dress Bldg., Wash., D.C.

36. National Home Study Council (Correspondence Schools and Courses)
839 17th St., N.W., Wash. 6, D.C.

37. National Kindergarten Association (Kindergarten-Primary Education)
8 W. 40th St., New York.

38. National Lead Co. (Art; Lead)
932 Wilson St., Los Angeles, Calif.

39. National Lime Association (Agriculture; Lime)
Wash. 5, D.C.

40. National Livestock and Meat Board (Nutrition)
407 S. Dearborn St., Chicago 5, Ill.

41. National Lumber Manufact. Association (Lumber)
1319 18th St., N.W., Wash. 6, D.C.

42. National Machine Tool Builders' Association (Machines; Tools)
10525 Carnegie Ave., Cleveland 6, Ohio.

43. National Metal Trades Association (Metals; Vocational Guidance)
122 S. Michigan Ave., Chicago 3, Ill.

44. National Municipal League (City Manager Plan)
299 Broadway, New York.

45. National Noise Abatement Council (Noise Abatement) *
9 Rockefeller Plaza, New York 20.

46. National Nursing Council for War Service (Nurses and Nursing)
1790 Broadway, New York 19.

47. National Occupational Conference (Vocational Guidance)
551 5th Ave., New York.

48. National Opinion Research Center (Elections; Public Opinion — Polls)
University of Denver, Denver, Colo.

49. National Paint, Varnish and Lacquer Association (Interior Decoration)
1500 Rhode Island Ave., N.W., Wash. 5, D.C.

50. National Park Association (National Parks and Reserves)
1214 16th St., N.W., Wash. 6, D.C.
51. National Peanut Council, Inc. (Peanuts)
812 Citizens and South National Branch Building, Atlanta, Ga.
52. National Planning Association (Aeronautics; Agriculture)
800 21st St., N.W., Wash. 6, D.C.
53. National Publicity Council for Health and Welfare Services, Inc. (Health; Hobbies)
259 Fourth Ave., New York 10.
54. National Recreation Association (Entertaining; Recreation)
315 4th Ave., New York 10.
55. National Rehabilitation Association (Disabled — Rehabilitation, etc.)
Box 1685, Roanoke, Va.
56. National Safety Council (Accidents — Prevention of; Safety Education; Traffic Regulations)
20 N. Wacker Drive, Chicago 6, Ill.
57. National Shrimp Canners and Packers Association (Fish (as Food))
Hibernia Bank Bldg., New Orleans 12, La.
58. National Soap Sculpture Committee (Handicraft; Soap Sculpture)
160 5th Ave., New York 10.
59. National Society Daughters of the American Revolution (Citizenship)
1776 D St., N.W., Wash. 6, D.C.
60. National Society for Crippled Children (Crippled Children; Palsy, Cerebral)
Elyria, Ohio.
61. National Society for Medical Research (Medical Research; Scientists)
25 E. Washington St., Chicago 2, Ill.
62. National Society for the Blind (Blind)
Woodward Bldg., Wash., D.C.
63. National Society for the Prevention of Blindness (Blind; Eye)
1790 Broadway, New York.

64. National Tuberculosis Association (Tuberculosis)
    1790 Broadway, New York 19.
65. National W.C.T.U. (Alcoholism)
    1730 Chicago Ave., Evanston, Ill.
66. Nehi Corporation (Clubs; Recreation)
    Columbus, Ga.
67. Neon Products, Inc. (Signs)
    Lima, Ohio.
68. Nevada University (Home Economics)
    Reno, Nev.
69. New American Library of World Literature, Mentor
    Books (General)
    245 5th Ave., New York 10.
70. New England Dairy and Food Council (Dairying;
    Milk)
    711 Boylston St., Boston, Mass.
71. New Hampshire University (Home Economics)
    Durham, N.H.
72. New Jersey State College of Agriculture (Agricul-
    ture; Home Economics)
    New Brunswick, N.J.
73. New Jersey Zinc Co. (Zinc)
    160 Front St., New York.
    New York State College of Agriculture. *See* Cornell
    University
74. New York State Museum (Birds)
    University of State of New York. Albany 1, N.Y.
75. New York Zoological Society (Animals; Fishes; Rep-
    tiles)
    Bronx Park, New York 60.
76. Northeastern Lumber Manufacturers Association
    (Lumber)
    271 Madison Ave., New York 16.
77. Northrup Aircraft, Inc. (Aeronautics)
    Hawthorne, Calif.
78. Northwestern Press (Dramas)
    2200 Park Ave., Minneapolis 4, Minn.
79. Nursing Information Bureau (Nurses and Nursing)
    1790 Broadway, New York 19.
80. Nystrom, A. J., and Co. (Maps)
    3333 Elston Ave., Chicago 18, Ill.

O

O. F. Mossberg. *See* Mossberg, O. F.

1. Oceana Publications (Inventions; Law)
   43 W. 16th St., New York 11.
2. Ohio Leather Co. (Leather)
   Girard, Ohio
3. Ohio Society for Crippled Children, Inc. (Crippled Children; Palsy, Cerebral)
   5 W. Broad St., Cleveland 15, Ohio.
4. Oil Industry Information Committee (Mines and Mineral Resources; Petroleum)
   50 W. 50th St., New York 20.
5. Operation America, Inc. (Subversive Activities)
   1120 Vermont Ave., N.W., Wash. 5, D.C.
6. Organization of American States, Pan American Union (Foreign Trade)
   17th St. and Constitution Ave., Wash. 6, D.C.
7. Oyster Institute of North America (Oysters)
   5600 32nd St., N.W., Wash. 15, D.C.

P

1. Palmer Match Co. (Matches)
   Akron, Ohio.
2. Pan American Coffee Bureau (Coffee)
   120 Wall St., New York 5.
3. Pan American Union (Latin America)
   19th St. & Constitution Ave., N.W., Wash., D.C.
4. Pan American World Airways System (Latin America)
   Educational Service, 28 Bridge Plaza, N., Long Island City 1, N.Y.
5. Park Publishing House (Vocational Guidance)
   4141 W. Vliet St., Milwaukee 8, Wisc.
6. Pemez Travel Club (Mexico)
   Juarez Ave. 89, P.O. Box 55 Bis, Mexico City, Mexico
7. Penguin Books (General)
   245 5th Ave., New York.

8. Penn, William, Publishing Corporation, Tudor Publishing Co. (Design)
   221 Fourth Ave., New York 3.
9. Pennsylvania Historic Association (Pennsylvania)
   Box 373, Gettysburg, Pa.
10. Pepperell Manufacturing Co. (Linen — Household)
    160 State St., Boston 2, Mass.
11. Pequot Mills, Educational Dept. (Linen — Household)
    Empire State Bldg., 350 Fifth Ave., New York 1.
    Peter Schauble and Associates. *See* Schauble, Peter, and Associates
12. Philco Corporation (Electronics)
    Tioga & C Sts., Philadelphia, Pa.
13. Piper Aircraft Corporation (Aeronautics)
    Lock Haven, Pa.
14. Pitney-Bowes, Inc. (Machinery)
    Walnut & Pacific Sts., Stamford, Conn.
15. Pittsburgh Plate Glass Co. (Glass Industry)
    6th Floor, 632 Duquesne Way, Pittsburgh 22, Pa.
16. Planters Nut and Chocolate Co. (Peanuts)
    632 S. Main St., Wilkes-Barre, Pa.
17. Plumbing and Heating Industries Bureau (Heating; Plumbing)
    35 E. Wacker Drive, Chicago, Ill.
18. Plymouth Cordage Co. (Rope)
    Plymouth, Mass.
19. Pocket Books, Inc. (General)
    1230 Ave. of Americas, New York 2.
20. Popular Mechanics Co. (Woodworking)
    200 E. Ontario St., Chicago 11, Ill.
21. Porter Chemical Co. (Atomic Energy; Chemistry)
    Hagerstown, Md.
22. Portland Cement Association (Cement Industry and Trade)
    33 W. Grand Ave., Chicago 10.
23. Poultry and Egg National Board (Poultry)
    308 W. Washington St., Chicago 6, Ill.
24. Prentice-Hall, Inc. (Business; Secretaries)
    70 Fifth Ave., New York 11.

25. Procter & Gamble Co. (Soap)
Cincinnati 1, Ohio.

26. Public Administration Service (Public Administration)
1313 E. 60th St., Chicago, Ill.

27. Publication Services (Young Women's Christian Association)
600 Lexington Ave., New York 22.

28. Purdue University (Agriculture; Home Economics)
Lafayette, Ind.

Q

Quarrie Corporation. *See* Field Enterprises

R

R. R. Bowker Co. *See* Bowker, R. R., Co.

1. R.C.A. Victor Division, Educational Services (Music)
Camden, N.J.

2. Radio Corporation of America, Dept. of Information (Electronics; Radio; Television)
30 Rockefeller Plaza, New York 20.

3. Rand, McNally & Co. (Flags; Maps)
536 S. Clark St., Chicago, Ill.

4. Ransdell, Inc. (General)
810 Rhode Island Ave., Wash., D.C.

5. Remington Rand (Files and Filing; Secretaries; Typewriting; Words)
315 Fourth Ave., New York 10.

6. Revere Copper and Brass, Inc. (Copper; Houses, Prefabricated)
230 Park Ave., New York 17.

7. Rit Products Corporation, Service Bureau (Color; Costume; Dyes and Dyeing)
1401 W. Jackson Blvd., Chicago 7, Ill.

8. Ross Allen's Reptile Institute (Reptiles)
Silver Springs, Fla.

9. Royal Crystal Sale Co. (Salt)
Salt Lake City, Utah.

10. Royal Typewriter Co. (Typewriting)
     2 Park Ave., New York 16.
11. Rudder Publishing Co. (Boats and Boating)
     9 Murry St., New York 7.

S

1. Saint Louis Post-Dispatch (United States — Constitution)
    St. Louis, Mo.
2. Salada Tea Co. (Tea)
    Salada Bldg., Stuart & Berkeley Sts., Boston, Mass.
    Samuel French, Inc. *See* French, Samuel, Inc.
3. Save the Redwoods League (Conservation of Resources)
    250 Administration Bldg., Univ. of Calif., Berkeley 4, Calif.
4. Schauble, Peter, and Associates (Capitalism)
    Haverford, Pa.
5. Schirmer, G., Inc. (Music)
    E. 43rd St., New York 17.
6. Scholastic Press (General)
    338 N.W. 9th Ave., Portland, Oregon.
7. Schroeder & Tremayne, Inc. (Sponges)
    1711 Delmar Blvd., St. Louis 3, Mo.
8. Science Associates (Weather)
    410 N. Broad St., Philadelphia 8, Pa.
9. Science Research Associates (Vocational Guidance)
    57 W. Grand Ave., Chicago 10.
10. Seahorse Press (Children's Parties)
     Pelham 65, N.Y.
11. Sears, Roebuck & Co. (Consumer Education)
     Consumer Education Division, Chicago 7, Ill.
12. Seth Thomas Clocks (Clocks and Watches)
     Thomaston, Conn.
13. Seventeen, Reader Service Dept. (Beauty, Personal; Vocational Guidance)
     488 Madison Ave., New York 22.
14. Sharp & Dohme (Health)
     640 N. Broad, Philadelphia 1, Pa.

15. Sherwin-Williams Co. (Interior Decoration)
    701 Canal Rd., N.W., Cleveland 1, Ohio.
16. Simmons-Boardman Publishing Co. (Marine Engines)
    30 Church St., New York.
17. Simmons College (Vocational Guidance)
    300 The Fenway, Boston 15.
18. Simon & Schuster, Inc. (General; Travel)
    1230 Sixth Ave., New York 20.
19. Singer Sewing Machine Co. (Sewing)
    Singer Bldg., New York 6.
20. Sky Publishing Co., Harvard College Observatory (Astronomy)
    Cambridge 38, Mass.
21. Society of the Plastics Industry (Plastics)
    295 Madison Ave., New York 17.
22. Sonotone (Ear)
    Elmsford, New York.
23. South Bend Lathe Works (Machinery)
    South Bend 22, Ind.
24. South Dakota State College of Agriculture (Agriculture; Home Economics)
    Brookings, S.D.
25. Southern Hardwood Producers, Inc. (Lumber)
    805 Sterick Bldg., Memphis 3, Tenn.
26. Southern Pine Assoc. (Lumber)
    New Orleans 4, La.
27. Southwestern Monuments Association (Flowers)
    Box 2011-U, Santa Fé, N.M.
28. Special Libraries Association (Library Science)
    31 E. 10th St., New York 3.
29. Sperry Gyroscope Co., Inc. (Gyroscope)
    Great Neck, New York.
30. Spool Cotton Co. (Crocheting; Knitting)
    745 5th Ave., New York.
31. Spratt's Patent Limited (Pets)
    Newark 5, N.J.
32. Standard Brands, Inc., Consumer Service Dept. (Coffee; Consumer Education; Cookery; Tea)
    595 Madison Ave., New York 22.

33. Standard Oil Co. (Conservation of Resources; Petroleum)
    30 Rockefeller Plaza, New York 20.
34. Stanford University, Graduate School of Business (Business; California)
    Palo Alto, Calif.
35. State College of Washington, Extension Service. (Agriculture; Consumer Education)
    Pullman, Wash.
36. Stechert-Hafner, Inc. (Language and Languages)
    31 E. 10th St., New York 2.
37. Sugar Research Foundation (Sugar)
    52 Wall St., New York 5.
38. Swift and Co. (Meat; Soap)
    Advertising Dept., Union Stock Yards, Chicago 9.
39. Switzerland Cheese Association (Cheese)
    105 Hudson St., New York.

T

1. Tanners' Council of America (Leather)
   100 Gold St., New York 7.
2. Taylor Instrument Co. (Weather)
   Rochester, New York.
3. Tea and Coffee Trade Journal (Coffee; Tea)
   79 Wall St., New York 5.
4. Tennessee University (Home Economics)
   Knoxville, Tenn.
5. Texas Gulf Sulphur Co. (Flowers; Insects)
   1002 Second National Bank Bldg., Houston 2, Texas.
6. Textile Foundation (Textiles; Vocational Guidance)
   Wash., D.C.
7. Town Meeting (General)
   32 S. 4th St., Columbus 15, Ohio.
8. Trailer Co. of America (Logistics; Trailers)
   31st St. & Robertson Ave. S., Cincinnati, Ohio.

U

1. Underwood Corporation (Typewriting)
   1 Park Ave., New York 16.

2. Underwriters Laboratories (Fire Protection)
   207 E. Ohio St., Chicago 11, Ill.
3. Union Carbide and Carbon Corporation, Bakelite Division (Plastics)
   300 Madison Ave., New York 17.
4. Union Fork and Hoe Co. (Gardening; Tools)
   Columbus, Ohio.
5. Union Pacific Railroad (Travel)
   1416 Dodge St., Omaha 2, Neb.
6. United Air Lines (Aeronautics)
   School and College Service, 80 E. 42nd St., New York 17.
7. United Fruit Co. (Fruit)
   Education Dept., Pier 3, North River, New York 6.
8. United Nations (United Nations)
   International Documents Service, Columbia University Press, 2960 Broadway, New York 27.
9. United Shoe Machinery Corporation (Shoes)
   140 Federal St., Boston, Mass.
10. United States Beet Sugar Association (Sugar)
    Wash. 5, D.C.
11. United States Rubber Co. (Rubber)
    1230 Sixth Ave., New York.
12. United States Steel Corporation (Steel)
    71 Broadway, New York 6.
13. United States Testing Corp. (Merchandising)
    Hoboken, N.J.
14. United Wallpaper Inc. (Wall Coverings)
    Merchandise Mart, Chicago 54.
15. Universal Handicrafts Service (Handicraft)
    1267 Sixth Ave., New York.
16. Universal School of Handicrafts (Handicraft)
    221 W. 57th St., New York.
17. University Museum (Art; Latin America)
    33rd & Spruce Sts., Philadelphia 4, Pa.
18. University of California, College of Agriculture (Agriculture)
    22 Giannini Hall, Berkeley 4, Calif.
19. University of Chicago, Round Table. Chicago, Ill. (General)

20. University of Illinois, College of Agriculture (Agriculture; Home Economics; Trees)
    Urbana, Ill.
21. University of Illinois, Library School (Library Science)
    Urbana, Ill.
22. University of Illinois Press (Salesmen and Salesmanship)
    Urbana, Ill.
23. University of Massachusetts (Games; Nature; Sports)
    Nature Education, Amherst, Mass.
24. University of Minnesota, Dept. of Agriculture (Agriculture; Trees)
    Agricultural Farm, St. Paul 8, Minn.
25. University of Missouri, College of Agriculture (Agriculture; Trees)
    Agricultural Extension Service, Columbia, Mo.
26. University of Oklahoma, Family Life Institute (Family Life)
    Norman, Okla.
27. University of Tennessee, Agricultural Experiment Station (Agriculture; Freezers and Freezing)
28. University of Washington, The Management Club (Salesmen and Salesmanship)
    Seattle, Wash.
29. University of Wisconsin, College of Agriculture (Agriculture; Trees)
    Madison 6, Wisc.
30. Updegraff Press (Public Relations)
    Scarsdale, New York.
31. Utah Agricultural College (Agriculture; Home Economics)
    Logan, Utah.

V

1. Veneer Association (Lumber)
   600 S. Michigan Ave., Chicago 5, Ill.
2. Vocation Information Services (Vocational Guidance)
   1235 Bates Road, Rocky River 16, Ohio.

3. Vocational Manuals, Inc. (Vocational Guidance)
45 W. 45th St., New York 19.

W

W. H. Baker. *See* Baker, W. H.

1. Waltham Watch Co. (Clocks and Watches)
Waltham, Mass.

Walton League of America, Inc. *See* Isaak Walton
League of America, Inc.

2. Warren Featherbone Co. (Cotton)
6 N. Michigan Ave., Chicago, Ill.

3. Washington Service Bureau (General)
1013 13th St., N.W., Wash., D.C.

4. Washington State Apple Commission (Apples)
Yakima, Wash.

5. Waterman's (Penmanship)
Broadway at Fulton, New York.

6. West Coast Lumbermen's Association (Lumber)
1410 S.W. Morrison St., Portland 5, Ore.

7. West Georgia College (Cookery)
Committee on Publications, Carrollton, Ga.

8. West Virginia University, College of Agriculture
(Agriculture; Trees)
Morgantown, W. Va.

9. Western Personnel Service (Vocational Guidance)
30 Raymond Ave., Pasadena 1, Calif.

10. Western Pine Association (Lumber; Woodworking)
Yeon Bldg., Portland 4, Ore.

11. Western Union Telegraph Co. (Telegraph)
60 Hudson St., New York 13.

12. Westinghouse Electric and Manufacturing Co. (Canning and Preserving; Cookery; Electric Apparatus
and Appliances; Freezers and Freezing; Laundry;
Vitamins)
246 E. 4th St., Mansfield, Ohio.

13. Westinghouse Electric Corporation (Teaching Aids)
School Service, 306 Fourth Ave., Pittsburgh 30, Pa.

14. Wheat Flour Institute (Teaching Aids; Wheat)
309 W. Jackson Blvd., Chicago 6, Ill.

15. White Sewing Machine Co. (Sewing)
    Education Dept., Cleveland 1, Ohio.
16. Whitman Publishing Co. (Animals; Birds; Dogs;
    Fishes; Flowers; Nature)
    1220 Mound Ave., Racine, Wisc.
17. Wilcox and Follet (General)
    1225 S. Wabash Ave., Chicago 5, Ill.
18. The Wild Flower Preservation Society, Inc. (Wild-
    flowers)
    3740 Oliver St., N.W., Wash. 15, D.C.
19. Wilderness Society (Birds; Conservation of Re-
    sources)
    1840 Mintwood Place, N.W., Wash. 9, D.C.
20. Wildlife Management Institute (Nature)
    709 Wire Bldg., Wash., D.C.
21. William-Frederick Press (General)
    313 W. 35th St., New York 1, N.Y.
    William Penn Publishing Corporation. *See* Penn,
    William, Publishing Corporation
22. Wilson, H. W., Co. (Library Science)
    950 University Ave., New York 52.
23. Woman's Day (Art; Woman)
    19 W. 44th St., New York 18.
24. Woman's Foundation (Family Life; Woman)
    10 E. 40th St., New York.
25. Woman's Press (Health; Parliamentary Practice;
    Woman)
    425 Fourth Ave., New York 16, N.Y.
26. Wool Bureau, Inc. (Wool)
    16 W. 46th St., New York 19.
27. Writer's Digest (Writing)
    22 E. 12th St., Cincinnati 10.

Y

1. Y.M.C.A. Bookstore (Young Men's Christian Association)
   5 W. 63rd St., New York 23.
   Y.W.C.A. *See* Publications Services

2. Yawman and Erbe Manufacturing Co. (Files and Filing)
   Rochester, N.Y.
3. York Band Instrument Co. (Musical Instruments)
   1600 Division Ave. S., Grand Rapids, Mich.

SUPPLEMENT III

SUBJECT INDEX TO "PARTIAL LIST OF ORGANIZATIONS, ETC. THAT ISSUE PAMPHLETS"

Number keys refer to numbers assigned to organizations, in Supplement II.

Subjects covered are representative only, rather than comprehensive.

Subject 　　　　*Number Keys*

A

Abrasives **B23**
Accidents — Prevention of **A113, F10, G14, M19, N56**
Accounting **M34**
Adult education **A19**
Advertising **A4, A5, A114, B25, C29, C36**
Aerodynamics **A90**
Aeronautics **A6, A8, A9, A10, A24, A109, B7, C55, G15, G16, N1, N52, N77, P13, U6**
Agricultural engineering **A82**
Agricultural machinery **A118, C12, C45, I6, M20**
Agriculture **A11, A103, C12, C19, C32, C47, F13, F16, G10, I11, K3, M7, M20, M26, N39, N52, N72, P28, S24, S35, U18, U20, U24, U25, U27, U29, U31, W8**
Air conditioning **C11**
Air pollution **B22**
Airports **N15**
Alcoholism **A65, N65**
Aluminum **A15, A16**
Animals **A68, A69, G1, L2, N75, W16**
Anthropology **C22**
Apples **W4**
Aquariums **D5**
Architecture **A55**
Art **A35, A107, B21, B36, D8, E11, F14, H12, N38, U17, W23**

Cards **A111**
Carpentry **H17, M10**
Catholic literature **C16**
Cats **A12**
Cattle **A17, A47, H15**
Cement industry and trade **P22**
Cereals **C18**
Cheese **K9, S39**
Chemistry **A33, A36, M8, P21**
Chemists **C48**
Chewing gum **A34, B8, F11**
Child study **A110, C24, G11, H8, I10**
Children's literature **C25**
Children's parties **S10**
Chinchillas **B13, N16**
Citizenship **N59**
City manager plan **N44**
City planning **A55, A84**
Clocks and watches **G22, S12, W1**
Clothing and dress **C29**
Clubs **N66**
Coal **A99, B22, H21, L6, N17**
Cocoa and chocolate **H11, L3**
Coffee **B38, P2, S32, T3**
Collective bargaining **A63**
Colonial life and customs **C31**
Color **A35, M28, R7**
Community chests **C39**
Conservation of resources **C12, D14, I14, S3, S33, W19**
Consumer education **C36, C43, D15, G7, H20, N19, N20, S11, S32, S35**
Cookery **C20, E12, G6, G19, K1, M16, N13, S32, W7, W12**
Copper **A97, C45, R6**
Corn **C46**
Corporations **N5**
Correspondence schools and courses **N36**
Costume **D6, R7**
Cotton **A91, B18, L16, N21, W2**
Cottonseed **N22**

Credit **D20**
Crime and criminals **A76**
Crippled children **N60, O3**
Crocheting **S30**
Cycling **B19**

D

DDT **C27**
Dairying **N23, N70**
Deaf **A81**
Dentistry **A37, B33**
Design **P8**
Diesel engines **D12**
Disabled — Rehabilitation, etc. **N55**
Disasters **A78**
Dogs **A12, J2, N24, W16**
Dramas **B1, D17, F20, N78**
Dyes and dyeing **M28, R7**

E

Ear **S22**
Economics **A4, C19, F19**
Elections **N48**
Electric apparatus and appliances **A86, E3, H19, I6, N25, W12**
Electronics **P12, R2**
Employees **A63**
Encyclopedias **C40, E8, F7, H6**
Engineering education **E9**
Entertaining **D6, N54**
Etiquette **A101**
Eye **B17, N63**

F

Factory management **A63**
Fairy tales **A39**
Family life **A57, F1, U26, W24**
Felt **A41**

Fertilizers **A18, M20, N29**
Files and filing **R5, Y2**
Fire protection **N11, N30, U2**
First aid in illness and injury **A78, B6**
Fish (as food) **G19, N57**
Fishes **A69, N75, W16**
Flags **A60, R3**
Floor coverings **A105, B20, C10, C28, F9**
Flowers **A69, G2, M9, S27, T5, W16**
Food **A51, A56, B24, B41, C2, C50, F16, G6**
Food — Canned **A30, H9, N13**
Foreign trade **O6**
Forests and forestry **A42, C15, F17**
Freezers and freezing **U27, W12**
Fruit **C2, C3, F22, U7**
Fuel **D2**
Furniture **A94, D21**

G

Games **A20, U23**
Gardening **U4**
Gardens **G2, N33**
Gas — Natural **A44**
General (Miscellaneous) **B3, B4, C23, C40, E4, E8, F7, G21, H16, L14, N69, P7, P19, R4, S6, S18, T7, U19, W3, W17, W21**
Geography **B15, H1, N34**
Geology **A45, C22**
Girl Scouts **G12**
Glass industry **P15**
Glassware **A46, C7, C48, F18**
Glue **L9**
Grain trade **M24**
Guns **M32**
Gyroscope **S29**

H

Handicraft **A49, A79, A106, A107, B39, D6, F5, F15, H2, H3, H18, N58, U15, U16**

L

Language and languages **S36**
Latin America **P3, P4, U17**
Laundry **A58, E2, G14, W12**
Law **A26, O1**
Lead **L5, N38**
Leather **O2, T1**
Leather work **A106, F5**
Libraries — Supplies **D4, G3**
Library science **A62, D18, F3, L17, S28, U21, W22**
Lime **N39**
Lincoln, Abraham **L13**
Linen — Household **C9, I12, K7, P10, P11**
Logistics **T8**
Lumber **A100, A102, C5, D16, M6, N41, N76, S25, S26, V1, W6, W10**

M

Machinery **B9, N42, P14, S23**
Management **A63**
Manufacturers **N5**
Maps **D7, H1, M3, N80, R3**
Marble **G9**
Marine engines **G20, S16**
Marriage **A51, A57, I3**
Matches **D10, P1**
Maternity welfare **M15**
Mathematics **B42**
Meat **A64, A104, S38**
Medical research **N61**
Merchandising **U13**
Metals **N43**
Meteors **A66**
Mexico **P6**
Microscopy **A71, B5**
Milk **M23, N70**
Milk, Evaporated **B24, E12**
Mimeographing **D11**
Mineralogy **C22, D9**

Shipping **N26**
Ships — Models **B29**
Shoes **F21, U9**
Signs **N67**
Silk **I9**
Silk, Artificial **A93, D21, N28**
Silver **H3**
Silverware **G18**
Smoke prevention **B22**
Soap **C30, F6, L10, P25, S38**
Soap sculpture **N58**
Social hygiene **A80**
Social work **A22, C39**
Socialism **C19**
Songs **A83**
Spices **A85, M1**
Spiders **A69**
Sponges **S7**
Sports **A20, B4, M32, U23**
Standardization **A86**
State governments **C49**
Steel **A13, A59, B16, U12**
Subversive activities **C37, O5**
Sugar **A88, C1, F2, G23, L16, S37, U10**
Swimming pools **A77**

T

Table **G18**
Taxation **A61, A89**
Tea **I13, M1, S2, S32, T3**
Teaching aids **A39, C40, C51, D22, E4, K8, L15, M11, M18, N5, W13, W14**
Telegraph **W11**
Telephone **B11**
Television **R2**
Textiles **A93, B36, B40, C17, D1, D21, N28, T6**
Thread **A91**
Tools **B9, D3, D13, G8, N42, U4**
Trade unions **A40, C41**

Traffic regulations **A23, I4, N56**
Trailers **T8**
Travel **B15, H4, H14, N34, S18, U5**
Trees **U20, U24, U25, U29, W8**
Tuberculosis **N64**
Typewriting **L1, R5, R10, U1**

U

Unemployment **C19**
United Nations **U8**
United States — Constitution **C34, S1**
Units of work **A107, B15**

V

Venereal diseases **H8**
Veterans **A60, C19**
Vitamins **A65, W12**
Vocational guidance **A9, A26, A32, A33, A38, B12, B26,
C6, G12, G13, G21, H16, I2, M5, M21, N43, N47,
P5, S9, S13, S17, T6, V2, V3, W9**

W

Wages **A63**
Wall coverings **I1, U14**
Water-supply **C13, C38**
Weather **E5, S8, T2**
Weeds **A69**
Welfare state **C19**
Wheat **W14**
Wildflowers **W18**
Williamsburg, Virginia **C31**
Wire **A87**
Woman **W23, W24, W25**
Woodworking **D3, H17, M10, P20, W10**
Wool **A95, B27, B28, N8, W26**
Words **F23, M17, R5**
Writing **A116, C8, W27**

Y

Yarn **B14, F12**
Young Men's Christian Association **Y1**
Young Women's Christian Association **P27**

Z

Zinc **A96, N73**
Zoology **C22**

INDEX